The Flip of a Coin

By J C Williams

ISBN-10: 1537392972
ISBN-13: 978-1537392974

First printing December 2014

Second printing October 2018

Third printing January 2020

Cover artwork by Paul Nugent

Formatting & interior design provided by Dave Scott and Cupboardy Wordsmithing

Dedication

To Fiona and Lucas,
for looking after me for three months.
And to the ruptured patella tendon,
for the time to write this book.

Chapter One

The intermittent flashing of the orange light attached to the top of the traffic cone had jarred Tom from a deep sleep several times during the night. In his confused, drunken state he'd mistakenly taken it to be an alarm clock and pressed down on it several times to operate the snooze function that didn't exist because, well, it was a traffic cone, after all. The three-foot garden gnome dressed as a Scottish highlander didn't appear overly impressed with the current situation, particularly due to fact that half of his nose was currently missing, and Tom hadn't dared to check beneath his impressive kilt to see if anything was also missing.

This was truly a mystery. Not the fact that he'd somehow acquired a traffic cone with flashing light, an oversized garden gnome, and what also appeared to be a painting of Winston Churchill (though it was difficult to make out in his hungover state, not to mention someone had drawn on with permanent marker a moustache, spectacles, and a Mohawk, muddying things further). No, the true mystery, as he sat with his back against the living room wall, was how he'd come home with the left leg of his trousers completely missing. It wasn't as if they'd been torn off in a frenzy, either. No, this was a precision removal that a seamstress would have been proud of. Confusing the situation further was the fact that he only had his right shoe… and that it was presently on his left foot. Little wonder, then, that he'd felt some discomfort from that area.

"Ahem," said Carol, standing over Tom with that what-*the-actual-hell-are-you-doing* expression etched in no uncertain terms over her face.

Tom glanced up to Carol and then to his other housemate, Mike, who stood a pace behind her and evidently on his way to work.

"Morning. I don't suppose there's any tea in pot, Carol?" said Tom. "And, you don't happen to know where *they* came from?" he said, pointing to the gnome and the traffic cone.

Carol was in her nurse's uniform, as petite as she ever was — no more than five-foot-three — but she looked concerned as she leaned toward him, grabbing him by the hands and pulling him to his feet.

Now he was standing upright, it was obvious to everyone how dishevelled he was. They could see that his trouser leg was missing but they'd yet to notice the absence of his shoe. Tom's black polo shirt was torn, revealing red marks on his chest. His styled black hair was unkempt, as was the stubble on his face. In contrast, Mike was dressed in an immaculate black suit with an open-necked white shirt and shoes that had evidently been polished with pride. Much taller than Tom, he looked over his thin-rimmed glasses and shook his head. "Tom, you are a mess!"

"Are you hurt?" asked Carol, as she walked around him, trying to look for any sign of injury.

Tom walked toward the black leather chair and sat with his back to the large sash window, his crooked posture flooded with light.

"No. Well, I don't think so. My head hurts a lot, though!"

Now Carol could see that there was no permanent damage, her face turned from compassion to frustration. She sat next to Tom and put her hand gently on his knee. "Tom, you have to stop this! You're thirty-five years old! You're emaciated, you're not eating right. I know I'm not your mother, but you should take a look at yourself!"

Tom ran his hands through his hair. "I know! I don't know what happened. I went out with a couple of the guys from work for a few pints, and then *this* — you two standing over me!"

"You staggered in at about two a.m.," said Mike. "You obviously don't remember waking me up to ask if I wanted a bit of your pizza or a whiskey?"

Tom shook his head and wondered what he'd done with the pizza box. He looked up at Mike and apologised, feeling a combination of nausea and remorse. Although he was no stranger to hangovers, this was a particularly bad one. But it wasn't just the hangover; he was also embarrassed that he couldn't remember coming home, and that it wasn't even the weekend yet! Blanking out for hours was the norm in his twenties, but what he dreaded most was the following day, when someone would inevitably relate to him his awful drunken behaviour from the night before.

He reached into his pocket and opened his wallet. It was empty.

Carol looked concerned again. "Were you robbed?"

"No, I only had twenty pounds in the first place. How did I get so drunk and order a pizza?"

"You were a bit down in the dumps as well, Tom, which isn't like you. You were mumbling your words a bit, but you told me you had a plan and that you were going to change."

"Did he mention Lou?" asked Carol.

"No, surprisingly not!"

Tom needed air, and moved toward the window, struggling to stop his hands from shaking. He looked outside and wondered what the plan was. He was frustrated that he couldn't remember anything, not even getting home. As he stood by the window, he noticed the discarded pizza box and half-empty bottle of whiskey, strewn by his feet. He assumed he had formulated his plan whilst looking out of the window onto the inspiring streets of Manchester, a plan he could no longer remember. "I need to start writing things down."

"Or cut down on your drinking!" suggested Mike. "I need to go to work. Don't forget— it's Friday!"

Mike picked up his black briefcase (which was the perfect complement to his suit), and despite it being a beautifully sunny day, reached for an umbrella. As he left, he looked very much the part of a steadfast accountant.

Tom and Mike were at two different ends of the spectrum. Mike was a career man, reliant on the regular paycheque, whereas Tom drifted between jobs and lived very much hand to mouth. Tom was grateful to Carol because few landlords were as understanding as she was when it came to late rent payments. Consequently, he didn't like leaving her without money, as she was more than just his landlord; she was his friend.

He often thought about how fortunate he was to live with Carol and Mike. They had been friends at high school but lost contact for years, and if it hadn't been for a chance meeting with Mike, there was no telling where he'd be now. He admired Carol for the way she had bettered her own life — she knew she didn't want to work in advertising, and she'd had the drive to retrain as a nurse. He tried to use her as his inspiration, but somehow he was frustrated. He knew he had to make a change but he didn't know what, or how.

Mike was a good friend, but as happens frequently with male friendships, he felt the need to project an air of bravado, or to create an illusion that he was happy with the trajectory his life was taking.

"I know you're right, Carol. I'm not a kid anymore and I have to snap out of this. I have to take control of my life and face up to responsibilities and really get my life on track!"

"Good, so are you going to work?"

"No. I'm going to phone in sick. I feel like shit!"

Despite his best intentions, Tom continued drinking over the weekend, but not to the excess of Thursday. He kept thinking about the drunken plan he had discussed with Mike.

Was it finally time to follow Carol's example and take control of his life?

This sense of initiative was unusual for him. The alcohol was acting as fuel for his determination. The next day, of course, normality would return, and those bold statements from the night before would be long forgotten.

Tom had read a quote and, unusually, it had struck a chord with him: "If you really want it, you will find a way. If you don't, you will find an excuse."

This was Tom. He was full of good ideas, but as soon as he faced any obstacles, he would use them as an excuse to justify failure.

Tom wanted something, but what, he did not know. Earlier in the year, he'd been invited to a careers convention at an e-gaming company. "I love poker, and the money is great!" he told Mike at the time. Mike asked him several days later how the new job was progressing.

"Ah, to be honest, Mike, it was on the other side of town. They wanted a full CV and references, which was a pain in the arse and I just didn't have time to get the paperwork together."

Tom ran through dozens of such examples in his head, but this particular one had struck a chord with him. *Did I really want this job?* he thought. *No,* he surmised, *If I wanted it, I would have got my arse on the train, written a CV, and done what everyone else does... make an effort!*

Tom did nothing about the job, and unsurprisingly, his life continued on the same track. It was a great source of frustration to him, and so he was determined to make a difference, to actually fulfil his goals, once and for all.

It was early on Sunday morning, earlier than his usual waking hours, and he felt fresh and energised, a feeling he had not enjoyed for as long as he could remember. He leapt out of bed and released a flurry of air punches like a boxer preparing for a fight. He ran his fingers through his hair and then released a couple of shots from his air pistols above his head.

Then he marched across the landing into Mike's room and announced: "I'm doing it, Mike, I'm doing it!"

"Great!" replied Mike, still half asleep. "What exactly are you doing?"

Tom didn't know, or certainly hadn't reached the point where he had a detailed plan. "Something, Mike! I don't know what, but it starts here!"

Mike had heard it before, and pushed an arm from under his warm duvet and raised his thumb in muted appreciation. "Great! You crack on, soldier!"

Tom was out there with a bold statement of intent, but the trouble was, he had no idea what he was going to do.

Carol and Mike would ask how his master plan was progressing, slightly tongue-in-cheek, but more to motivate rather than to tease.

Tom was inspired by a man who lived his life by the flip of a coin. He had seen him on a documentary, and he would make life decisions based on how the coin landed. It was a dramatic way to live, but Tom could appreciate that decisions would be made, whatever the outcome.

The weeks since he made his bold announcement flew by, and Tom was now in the middle of summer, yet he still hadn't done anything. The initial enthusiasm had started to wane, and his housemates could see the spiral starting all over again. He would drink straight from work, and that smart-but-scruffy appearance of his had simply turned to scruffy.

The only positive in his life was that he enjoyed working in a bookmakers, and figured that if he was working in one then he wasn't spending in one.

He kept thinking about the man who flipped the coin, and in his head he knew he had to do something now, before summer finished. Those dark nights of winter would do little for his motivation.

It was early evening on a Friday. Carol sat in the front room on the large black leather sofa, and was startled to hear the door opening. Mike was at a works function, and it couldn't be Tom because it was Friday and it was early.

The front door opened directly onto the living room, and Carol was surprised — and pleased — to see a sober-looking Tom. His stubble was neat, and he was smartly dressed in jeans with a white short-sleeved shirt that from where she sat appeared to have been ironed. Carol was slightly taken aback as she looked at him standing in the doorway. For a moment, she thought he looked handsome.

Carol felt vulnerable because she was dressed in shorts and a scruffy grey-hooded fleece, since she incorrectly assumed that she would have the house to herself. Despite the relaxed appearance, her blonde bobbed hair was neat, and her stylish black glasses could not hide her piercing blue eyes.

Tom smiled, as he often did when he saw Carol. He had a strange look on his face and Carol looked puzzled, unsure if it was a happy face or not.

"I quit my job today!" announced Tom proudly.

Carol leaned forward on the sofa and looked surprised as she puffed out her cheeks. "Brilliant. So, rent? How does that one work?"

Tom walked toward her and sat on the lone chair opposite her. In truth, he hadn't thought about all of the practicalities. He just knew that the weeks were passing, and if he didn't do something, nothing would happen. He had, in essence, mentally flipped a coin, and that coin said that he needed to quit work. It made sense to him because if he carried on working at the bookies, nothing would change. At least by quitting his job, he would be forced to do or at least attempt something different.

"Tom, I am all for you doing something, but you need a plan," stressed Carol, looking stern. "We all have a shit day and dream of jacking it all in to do something different. The difference is we have responsibilities. It's part of being an adult. We don't quit our jobs on a whim. I trained for years to become a nurse. I did that so I could quit my shit job in advertising and do something I wanted to do. I did this because I had responsibilities. What about you? Are you having some premature midlife crisis?"

Tom looked down at his feet. He knew that outwardly he looked like a petulant child sulking in his room, but he was listening to Carol. What Carol was saying were things he had considered but quickly discounted. Tom had developed the remnants of a plan, and part of that plan was to remove obstacles that would get in the way, such as his job.

"I will get you the money, Carol. I would never leave you in the shit."

Carol walked over to Tom and put a gentle hand on his shoulder. "I know you wouldn't, Tom, but it isn't about the money. I want you to be happy, and I'm pleased you're doing something about it, but please, think about it. I don't want to sound like your mum, but I could honestly shake you at times!"

"I know, Carol, and I know what I'm going to do."

Carol was trying to be positive and didn't want to shatter his plans, no matter how ill-conceived. "Oh, and what is that?"

Tom had not counted on having to explain his plan at this point, simply because he still didn't have one. A thousand thoughts ran through his head, but he knew if he did not commit now, he was going back to a dead-end job, no money and ambling through life.

He stared blankly at Carol, but try as he might, there was nothing there; his head was empty. The only thing he could think of was their small family business back in Tinsbury, the place he'd escaped from two years before.

"I'm going home, to help on the campsite. I spoke with my brother, Ricky, and he said he was struggling and could do with a bit of help, and as I was between jobs I could head back to help him out for a bit."

Carol looked decidedly underwhelmed, but at the same time did not want to dampen the enthusiasm.

"Okay," said Carol, "at least you know what you're doing. When are you going?"

"Monday!" he quickly replied.

He hadn't even thought about this, and didn't even have the cash to book a train to get back home. He briefly flirted with the idea of asking Carol for a small loan, but thought better of it.

Carol looked surprised. "Wow, it's Friday today. That was quick. You know we'll miss you, don't you?"

Carol didn't for a moment believe that he was going, certainly not in a few days, but by playing along she was calling his bluff. She didn't want him to leave, but she was intrigued as to how this charade was going to play out. It was like an adult pandering to a child who had threatened to leave home for the first time.

"Oh, what did your boss say?" she asked.

Tom shook his head. "Nothing yet. He hasn't texted me back."

Carol shook her head and rolled her eyes.

Tom hadn't intended for one minute to go back home, as he had left there for a reason, and all those reasons were flooding back to him. He also knew there was no chance of getting his old job back, as the garage had closed. He had worked at his Uncle Harry's garage for years, but since he left, the business continued to slow down, and his Uncle wasn't getting any younger.

Tom knew that career opportunities in a rural village were hard to come by, as most businesses were family-run, and people tended not to move onto new jobs.

The only option he could think of was to work on his mum's campsite. His dad had died several years before, and his mum ran the campsite with the help of his dad's friend, Paul.

Tom's brother, Ricky, was technically the manager, but he wasn't the brightest, and without his mother's oversight, the place would have folded years ago.

The campsite was essentially three fields with a shower block and a few additional camping huts. It had always been relatively busy, as it was situated at the heart of the picturesque village of Tinsbury, and had the benefit of a village pub less than a five-minute walk away. Tinsbury and the surrounding areas were stunning, and people returned each year to take advantage of the tranquil surroundings.

Like the majority of children, Tom didn't appreciate the village as he grew up. It was only as an adult that he realised how fortunate he had been to grow up in such a beautiful and safe environment.

As Monday rapidly approached, Tom started to panic. He hadn't booked his train, as he still had no money, but more importantly, he had yet to phone his mum and tell her he was coming home. He was confident she would be pleased, but he'd been gone for two years. Would she want him moving back in with her?

It was Sunday midmorning, and Tom was pacing the living room as Mike sat eating his breakfast. Tom was pretending to look interested in something through the front window, but it was clear to Mike that he was trying to build up the courage to ask him something, or at least waiting for the right time. It was a look that Mike had only seen whenever Tom was looking to borrow something, usually money.

Tom waited for a few moments and turned around with purpose and a smile on his face. "Is there any chance you can lend me some cash? I hate to ask, but I'm supposed to be going tomorrow and I haven't even got the train fare!"

Mike had to laugh. "You're leaving tomorrow and you haven't even got the train fare? Why don't you stick it on your credit card?"

Mike had heard Tom on the phone with a credit card company earlier in the day, and laughed as he listened to Tom give a vague promise to make a minimum payment as soon as he could.

Tom appreciated the humour, and gestured a pair of scissors with his fingers over an imaginary credit card.

"Do you want me to give you a lift?"

Tom smiled broadly, and secretly hoped that Mike would offer. "You do know it's a two-hour drive to Tinsbury?"

"That's fine. It'll give me a chance to get out of the city for a while. Plus, I'm off next week, so I would just be scratching around here anyway."

"Ah, legend, that would be amazing. Any chance you can phone my mum for me as well?"

"You're pathetic, man, just phone her and get it done. The only other option is to turn up with your suitcase!"

Tom spent the rest of the morning sorting his stuff out, and for once he was organised and had packed his bags in advance. As he threw them into the back of the plush Mercedes, he couldn't help but feel underwhelmed by his worldly possessions.

He looked at Mike and pointed toward his bags. "This is it, the sum total of my life!"

He was thirty-five, and everything he owned fitted into two holdalls and a backpack. He chose not to dwell on this, and instead took the lack of belongings as a positive, as he didn't have much to carry.

Carol stood in the doorway of her modest three-bedroom terraced house, watching Tom and knowing she would miss him a great deal. The money had been useful, but more than that, she had grown fond of him. He could be frustrating, but like Mike, she admired his approach on life and had been somewhat surprised by his current determination. She did wonder if more structure in his life would change the person he was. Secretly, she thought that life back home would be no different or offer anything more than he currently had, but that was something that Tom would need to figure out for himself.

She grabbed her coat and shouted to Tom: "Come on, then, we're taking you down The Saddle for a few farewell beers!"

The three housemates took the short walk to the pub, which had been their local for the last two years. It was a walk they'd taken dozens of times, but this time Tom felt a little flat. Carol snuggled into him and wrapped herself under his coat. Mike walked slightly behind them, and also felt a little flat, as he knew things wouldn't be quite the same without Tom.

The Saddle was a cosy pub with steep steps to the entrance, which always presented difficulty at closing time. The door was a heavy glass door, which took some effort to open. The force used on the door would always make the locals turn to see who'd entered. It was unusual to have such a rustic style pub so close to the city, but people enjoyed it, and no matter what day it was there was always a great atmosphere. It was relatively small inside, so finding a table was often a luxury, but as it was early afternoon they were able to get a seat next to the window.

Carol and Mike were surprised, as Tom took the short walk to the bar and bought a round of drinks. Tom didn't always have cash but when he did he was generous, often over-generous, which usually accounted for money slipping through his fingers so quick. He placed the drinks on the table with a huge grin on his face.

Mike picked up his drink and took a grateful mouthful. "Someone's happy!"

Tom rubbed his hands in delight. "Five draws on the fixed odds coupon, you little beauty!" He pulled out a pile of notes from his pocket and counted out the remaining rent he needed to give to Carol. He felt great; he hated owing people money. Credit card companies, on the other hand, he wasn't in such a rush to pay.

Carol smiled and shook her head. "I bet you spent the last of your cash to win this?"

Tom smiled and deliberately skipped over the question by raising a toast. "To good friends, good company and good people!"

Carol reached into her bag. "I bought you a present. Well, two actually!"

Tom looked genuinely pleased, and gave Carol a peck on the cheek as he tore the paper off one of the presents, revealing a book inside. It was called *Your Best Life Now*, by Joel Osteen.

"A cheesy American self-help book," said Carol with a smile. "If they can't help you out, Tom, no one can!"

Tom opened the other present with a huge grin. "A magic 8-ball! I used to love these things! Thanks, Carol." He smiled as he furiously shook his new present. "Will I ever wake up next to Carol?"

He sighed as the 8-ball fell into its resting position: *NOT LIKELY*.

Carol frowned. "Sorry, Tom, but it never lies!"

Mike returned from the bar with another round of drinks. "So will you get a new housemate, Carol?"

"I'm not sure, to be honest. The money helps, but it'll be nice to have a bit more room in the house, plus one less set of pubes in the shower is quite appealing." She said this casting an accusing glance at Tom. "I'll see how it goes, but if Tom's midlife crisis doesn't pan out, I might keep the room open for him."

"So, is being a nurse all you hoped for?" asked Mike. "Are you up to your elbows in shit and vomit every day?"

Carol nodded. "Yes, but being covered in shit and vomit is better than working in advertising!"

"Yeah, but the money was good, wasn't it?"

"Better than being a nurse, but I was surrounded by wankers, working for wankers!"

Mike nodded. "Sounds a bit like accountancy, to be honest!"

"At least you did something about it, Carol," stressed Tom. "Mike will be an office monkey until he pulls his pension."

"Shit, you could be right," groaned Mike. "Ask the 8-ball."

"Will Mike be a number-crunching office jockey till he dies?" asked Tom, shaking his new toy. He slowly looked up at

Mike. "As long as you wear those stupid glasses with that stupid briefcase, absolutely!"

The drinks continued into the evening, and Tom enjoyed it, but it was tinged with sadness at the thought of leaving. He would only be a couple of hours away, but he knew from experience that promises to keep in touch were rarely followed through. He had only phoned home a handful of times, and that was to his mum. What hope did he have of keeping in touch with Mike and Carol?

The three housemates called it a day, and Tom took one last look at The Saddle, which had been the scene of some fantastic nights out.

"I won't miss those bloody stairs!" he shouted, as he slipped and struggled to remain upright.

He stood in the middle of Mike and Carol, and put his arms around each of them, not knowing when he would next have the opportunity.

It was quiet, but he enjoyed the peace, and was enjoying the short walk back to the small terraced house that he had called home for the last two years.

Carol leaned forward and looked over to Mike. "I meant to ask, number boy, who was that girl you brought home on Friday? She wasn't exactly quiet!"

It was dark but it was clear that Mike was blushing, as he deliberately changed the subject.

There was a temptation to carry on drinking when they got back to the house, but Tom wanted to be reasonably fresh for the journey home, and certainly didn't want to be in the car for two hours with a raging hangover.

He struggled to sleep that night, and awoke early, apprehensive and nervous. His mind was racing with self-doubt. *What the hell am I doing?* he thought. *I'm going back to live with my mum. I'm thirty-five. I'll see that dickhead Lou and her new bloke. No proper job. I'll be telling campers to turn their music down, and emptying shit from communal toilets.*

The doubt was like an unattended car alarm in his head, and it was a new concept to him, as usually he gave little regard to consequences. At the very least, it was like a distant voice at the back of his head. He walked into the front room where Mike was eating his breakfast. "Mike, am I doing the right thing here?"

Mike was not used to seeing Tom so serious, and he now appeared riddled with self-doubt. Acknowledging that his friend seemed troubled, Mike gave the question due consideration.

"Don't be a twat," he finally said. "You go, it doesn't work out, and you come back!"

Tom looked a little relieved, and was pleased to hear the reassurances. "What about Lou and Pete? I don't want them thinking I'm some sort of loser."

Mike continued to eat his breakfast without breaking his stride. "Fuck them! What have they done for the last two years, ambled along in their dead-end jobs, probably spat out a kid? Don't worry about them, worry about you!"

Tom gave Mike a gentle punch on the shoulder. "Aww, mate, thanks!"

Tom had given a lot of thought to Lou and Pete, and he would have loved to have returned to the village with a stunning blonde on his arm in an expensive sports car. But it wasn't him, and he would have to manage with what he had, which wasn't a lot.

He got the last of his bits together and gestured Mike to hit the road. This was the moment he had been dreading, as he gave Carol a warm embrace.

Carol held back a tear and in a broken voice gently threatened him. "You stay in touch or I'll remove your bollocks! I'm a nurse, I know how."

Tom smiled and walked to the car, giving one final look back at Carol, who was waving from the front room window. He blew a kiss as the car pulled slowly away.

Chapter Two

The drive back to the country took them through the business district of Manchester, and Tom looked at the hordes of people heading into the office for a day of work. "Look at them, Mike, they look like ants. The amount of suits that used to come in the bookies and spend serious cash, you wouldn't believe!"

"What sort of cash, hundreds?"

"And the rest, mate! There were three lads, probably in their early twenties, who used to drop thousands a week. Probably merchant bankers earning six figures a year, but still, they were losing fortunes."

"It's all relative," replied Mike. "The more you earn, the more you spend, or in this case, gamble. We get it in our place. You see the bank statements for some of these guys and they are pissing thousands away. People you think are minted are skint. It's all on tick and credit cards."

"My old boss at the bookies used to love these flash little twats with a few quid on the hip," said Tom. "It always started out low-key, with a couple of hundred here and the odd win. But Larry wasn't stupid, because he would give the good punters a tab and make them feel important. He knew that if people came in with a hundred in cash then the chances were that's all they'd spend, whereas if they had a tab, they'd get out of their depth quickly. They would chase their losses and keep going. If you're pulling hard cash out of your pocket, you know how much you're spending, whereas ask me to stick it on their tab and they lose track. Larry was harmless-looking and an absolute gent, but my god, if you owed him money, he was a nightmare. Those three lads, the bankers, were into him for a fortune in the end. I don't know how much, as they started going to his card games as well as dropping cash on the horses. They started hitting the bottle and snorting the good stuff, and before long they get sacked from work and the big paycheques dry up. Then they stop phoning Larry back, and he is the sort of guy you don't ignore."

Mike looked a little surprised. "Is this not the guy you told to stick his job, by text message?"

"Yeah, but we got on and I didn't owe him money! I was a good worker for him and he said I could have a job back whenever."

"So what did he do to those three lads?"

"No idea, to be honest, but Larry was driving one of their cars a few days later so I'm guessing they came to an amicable settlement. Larry was never stupid enough to throw a punch. He would turn up at their work and stand outside their offices or knock on their door at night when their wives, friends, or mum were in. They would be in some wine bar and Larry would turn up with a smile on his face. The guys knew Larry was a nutcase, but he would use the psychological approach, which had always worked for him. Why throw a punch when you don't need to?"

The depressing, grey buildings of the city soon disappeared and were replaced with the tranquil, serene beauty of the countryside. In spite of his time living in Manchester, he was desperate to immerse himself in the limitless, rolling green hills that he was proud to call home.

Mike was also absorbed with the view, and was pleased he'd offered to drive Tom. "When are you officially in the countryside? You know, instead of being in the city?"

"When you see John Craven with his hand up a cow's ass!" explained Tom.

"Ah! Hopefully business rather than pleasure?"

Tom felt relaxed as he wound the window down to absorb the country air. "I love it out here. It's just peaceful. Nothing is rushed."

"Has your mum always had the campsite?"

"My dad's family were farmers, and when things slowed down they looked for other options to make money from the land, so my dad set up the campsite when I was only a kid. It was great growing up around a campsite because Ricky and I would have an endless supply of new friends, but the only problem was that they were usually gone after a few days. You used to get the same families coming back year on year, which was good. There were always a few girls, which was always a bonus! Mum hasn't said too much, but I get the impression that things are not as busy as they were. Well, what would you rather do, jump on the plane for a week in the sun, or sit in a piss-wet field?"

"Maybe leave the marketing to your brother," suggested Mike. "So what are you going to do if your brother is running the place?"

"Mum's looking to take a step back, so this will be her ideal opportunity."

"Does she actually know this, though?"

"Not yet," smiled Tom. "But Ricky is taking care of the bookings and stuff. I'll help out with the maintenance and day-to-day things, plus keep an eye on Ricky. I've got a few ideas to drum up a bit of business and see if I can bring a bit of extra cash in."

"Legal, though?" asked Mike.

Tom laughed. "Some of it!"

Tom smiled as they drove past an imposing set of large, cast-iron gates with a large mansion barely visible beyond the trees. "Conker heaven when we were kids that place."

"The old boy went nuts when we used to sneak in there. He used to run out of the house threatening to shoot us. Jesus, we were only kids. You'd call the cops if someone threatened you with a gun now. One day, the old boy came driving up the lane and Ricky hadn't seen him coming. Me and a few of the other lads had seen him, and jumped behind something. Ricky just carried on picking up conkers. I shouted over to him to run, and he must have heard the panic in my voice. Ricky ran, alright— he didn't even look as he went straight into the path of the old boy's car. He was okay, but he got a fair old wallop. The daft thing is we didn't even come out from behind the bush, as we didn't want to get shouted out. The old boy took Ricky home and Mum shit herself. There was nothing broken, but he wasn't quite the same after that, a little slower. Modem rather than broadband, if you know what I mean."

The main road quickly turned into a country road surrounded on all sides by tall trees that seemed to form an arch in front of them. It was dark from the canopy of trees blocking most of the natural light. Mike slowed down, nervous that they would meet oncoming traffic. "All this bloody space, you'd think they'd make the roads a bit wider!"

The trees soon gave way to vast open countryside, and they quickly reached the sign announcing their arrival in Tinsbury. Although they had been friends at school, Mike had never been to Tinsbury, and he was overwhelmed by the view before him. "This is stunning!"

Tom agreed, and felt a sense of pride, introducing an outsider to his home. The village was something from a postcard, a village you'd see in *Midsummer Murders*. It was a cliché of rural England. It was a different world, only two hours from Manchester, but it could have been on a different planet. Mike drove past cottages with golden thatched roofs and ivy crawling up the walls and it felt like any stress from the city was being cleansed. He virtually stopped the car, arching his neck as he appreciated the beauty of the village.

Mike was surprised as people walking through the village greeted them with a friendly wave. Everything just appeared quaint: the village shop, the church, the village green. Everything looked like it had been crafted to add to the character of the village, rather than being tacked on haphazardly.

"Turn right after the bridge," indicated Tom.

Mike noticed the village pub, which like the other buildings in the village was simply stunning, with a stream running through the side of the property. It was a typical country village pub with its cream façade warmly embraced in dark oak beams, and it was the sort of building that just invited you in.

"The Abbots Bridge," explained Tom. "A great little pub and always good for a lock-in! The landlord is a guy called Sammy Pope, nice bloke but drinks more than he sells, and always falling asleep at the end of the bar."

A short distance up the road there was a large sign with a tent indicating their arrival at the campsite. "This is it. Take the next turning on the left."

Mike pulled the car into a small gravel driveway and looked up at the modest detached house. It looked out of place with the village, and Mike was surprised that it was located on such a small plot considering the amount of available space.

Tom's mum, Linda, had heard the car arrive, and walked quickly toward them, giving Tom a warm embrace.

Mike had spoken to Linda plenty of times but had never met her in person. He had formed an image in his mind of what she looked like, but he was surprised. He'd expected her to be formal, bordering on posh, but she was nothing of the sort. She was dressed in white linen trousers with a smart floral shirt, and looked younger than he'd thought. He felt a tinge of guilt because he looked at her long brown hair and pretty face, and found her quite attractive.

He stepped out of the car. "Great to finally meet you, Linda! What a stunning village!"

"Yes, it's great, and if you carry on up the road it gets even better. There's a large water sports centre on the reservoir, and the scenery up there is amazing. Hopefully you can have a look around before you head back. Are you going to stay over before you head back, Mike?"

Mike shrugged his shoulders and looked toward Tom. "I hadn't really thought about it, to be honest."

Tom nodded. "Go on Mike, you don't need to head back to work tomorrow. Plus, we can get a blessing from the Pope down the pub."

Mike was slightly surprised, as he got the impression from Tom that he didn't really get on with his mum. Mike had assumed that she would be cold and maybe a bit distant but that didn't seem to be the case. She appeared warm and friendly.

Mike followed Linda into the house. "You can tell me all about Tom as a kid. Maybe dig some old favourite photographs out for us?"

Tom walked into the house and it became apparent that Paul had moved in. He didn't need to be Columbo to spot the men's shoes and coat hung behind the door. Tom liked Paul, but the fact that he was his dad's best friend had never sat well with him. A long time had passed since his dad had died and he understood that his mum had to move on.

Tom looked into the sitting room. "Where's Ricky?"

"If he isn't in there, he's probably down at the office. Why don't we enjoy this tea, take a walk down there, and I'll show you where you're staying! Mike you can either bunk in with Tom or sleep in the house if you're staying over, whatever you'd be comfortable with?"

Linda poured the tea and looked at Tom suspiciously. "So what brings you back, then, Tom? Women, or money, or both?"

Tom looked at Mike with his mouth wide open, pretending to be hurt. "I missed you all."

Linda let out a loud laugh, but it was clear it was meant with affection. "Rubbish! Mike, did he get someone pregnant?"

Mike put his hands in the air. "Leave me out of this one!"

Linda placed a hand on Tom's shoulder. "Well, whatever the reason, I'm glad to see you. Would it have killed you to pick the phone up more often?"

"I've got about two years' worth of washing in the back of the car to keep you busy."

"He's not joking, Linda, you should have smelt his bedroom!"

Linda smiled at she pointed to the washing machine. "At thirty-five years old, if you think I'm doing your washing, you can think again!"

"How are things around here?" asked Tom. "I get the impression from Ricky that business is a bit slow?"

"Slow!" said Linda. "He's being somewhat generous with that. It's busy at the weekends and when the weather is nice, but really quiet during the week. Ricky's doing his best, but I'm sure he'd appreciate your help."

Tom couldn't help but notice that his mum looked tired, and suspected it was from worrying about the business. "Is Ricky coping with the work?"

"There isn't that much to do, to be honest," said Linda. "He is managing, but you need to keep an eye on him, Tom. I do worry about him at times. People try and rip him off, tell him they've been here for three days instead of four, that sort of thing. It's not a lot, but it adds up. He paid hundreds to put a full-page advert in the local paper. It's a local paper for god's sake! The people around here already know about us, it's everyone else who we need to attract. His heart is in the right place. Will you keep an eye on him, Tom?"

Tom nodded reassuringly. "Of course I will, Mum." He knew that Ricky did everything with good intentions, as there wasn't a bad bone in his body. Those that knew him appreciated him for it, but those that didn't would often take advantage of his good nature.

"If you ever need help with the books, Linda, I'd be happy to help."

She smiled. "That's very kind, Mike, and we may take you up on that. Let's finish these, and we'll walk down to see Ricky."

Mike felt a little uneasy encroaching on the family reunion, but Linda made him feel very welcome. He dropped back slightly as mother and son linked arms. As they turned into the campsite, Mike was surprised at how big it was. There was a large field, which looked like it had at one time been two separate fields, as there were remnants of a small dividing wall on the far side. In the distance the site extended into an L-shape with the remainder of the site not visible from the entrance area. A tarmac road ran through the length of the site to allow vehicle access and avoid the field getting dragged up in wet weather.

The backdrop was stunning, and the campsite was covered on all sides with beautiful rolling hills. Mike stood in awe and could understand why people would return time and time again to appreciate this view. Everywhere he looked it was green; it was a view he would never tire of admiring.

An attractive red cedar log cabin had a large welcome sign with instructions for all visitors to check in before pitching their tent. Beside the cabin was a slide and swings on a bed of wood chippings. Mike was surprised, as he didn't know what to expect, but the site was big, clean and looked like a professional set up. Tom had always been a bit disorganised and he had incorrectly assumed the family business would be operated in the same manner.

A vehicle came speeding toward them. As it got closer, Mike could see that it was a golf cart, or rather a golf cart painted in army camouflage. As the cart pulled alongside them, Mike noticed that in addition to the paint, wide wheels and alloys had also been fitted. He smiled. He'd never seen a golf cart modified in such a way.

Tom walked toward the cart and waved. "Ricky," he said, as he warmly embraced his brother.

Mike was astonished as a huge lump of a man climbed out of the golf cart. Ricky must have been over 6 foot tall and was barrel-chested. He wasn't fat, just well-built, which gave him the appearance of carrying a little extra weight, and with a closely shaved haircut, he gave off a slightly intimidating impression. He was dressed in ripped green combat shorts and a vest-style white shirt. He gave every appearance of someone you would cross the road to avoid, and Mike couldn't help but imagine him working on a farm in the Australian outback. Ricky was younger than Mike, so he had left high school when Ricky was there.

Ricky walked over with a huge smile, and picked up the slightly-built Tom in a warm bear hug embrace. "Welcome back, Tom!"

Tom pretended to gasp for breath. "Good to see you, buddy, love the wheels! This is Mike."

Ricky extended a warm handshake. "Ah, the accountant. Nice to meet you, Mike."

Mike was confused, as Tom and Ricky were nothing like each other, and he briefly wondered if his mum had been friendly with Paul earlier than most people suspected.

Ricky ushered them with his shovel-like hands. "Come on, I'll show you around."

Linda waved goodbye and walked back to the house. "I'll leave you boys to it. Let me know if you want any food?"

Mike knew he shouldn't, but he couldn't resist looking at Linda as she turned onto the road back to the house.

Ricky patted the dashboard of his golf cart proudly. "I've tuned her up as well."

Tom wondered how you could tune up a golf cart, and his question was quickly answered as Mike nearly fell out of the back as Ricky pressed the accelerator.

Tom laughed loudly. "Shit, this thing's quick! You nearly killed Mike!"

Ricky accelerated over to the far end of the field on the newly-tarmacked access route. There was a large wooden building, which had not been visible from the entrance. The building looked newly built, but the colour of the wood complimented the tranquil surrounding.

Tom pointed to the building. "Jesus, where did that come from?"

Ricky looked proudly. "Not bad, is it!"

Ricky pulled up next to the new building and brought Tom and Mike inside. There were two doors with one leading to a large games room and the other leading to an ultra-modern toilet and shower block.

Tom was shocked at the extent of the changes since he had last been home. "Those toilets are better than most hotels I've stayed at!"

Ricky stood looking like a proud father. "The tarmac goes the length of the campsite. We were getting a lot of campervans, which were ripping up the grass. I also put twenty electric hook-up points in as well."

Mike now had full visibility of the site, and was even more impressed, but he couldn't help but notice that there was nobody there; certainly no campervans. "Is it slow during the week, Ricky?"

Ricky looked dejected. "Very! I tried a bit of advertising last month to drum up some business, but nothing."

"Yeah, Mum said," replied Tom, consciously trying to be positive. "Did you think about advertising a bit further away, rather than the local paper?"

Ricky stared at Tom. As he didn't know Ricky, Mike wasn't sure if the man's expression was one of blank neutrality or brotherly aggression. After a pause, Ricky let out a loud laugh and slapped Tom on the back. "Good one!" he said, leaving Mike and Tom with confused looks on their faces.

Tom looked at Mike and shrugged his shoulders. "Fair play, Ricky. What you've done here is amazing. The place looks fantastic!"

Tom wasn't trying to humour Ricky; he was genuinely impressed. Ricky had always been a hard worker and good with manual work, but the extent of his achievement came as a big surprise. Mike nodded in agreement.

"Ricky, are you okay with me coming back?"

Ricky smiled. "Of course I am. Over the moon, to be honest!"

Tom appreciated that response because it had been playing on his mind. "Don't think I'm here to try and take over or boss you around, Ricky, because I am not."

"Oh, I know! A bit of help would be good, to be honest. You can take care of the phone and the bookings. People keep getting pissed off and shouting at me!"

"No problem, Ricky. We'll get our heads together, see if we can't drum up a bit of business as well!"

Ricky was pleased to have Tom back, as although he'd appreciated the responsibility given to him, he'd struggled. He enjoyed the physical aspect of the job, particularly the recent renovations, but he did not enjoy the actual business side of things.

Tom climbed cautiously back into the golf cart. "Come on, I'll take us for a pint!"

"You've actually got money?" asked Ricky.

"Yeah, crazy isn't it? Courtesy of a little win at the bookies. We need to drum up some business, Ricky, so I can get paid."

"Yeah, me too!" laughed Ricky.

Tom looked concerned at Ricky's flippant response. "You aren't getting paid?"

Ricky didn't appear concerned. "No, not for months. It's all gone on the renovations."

Shit, thought Tom.

Tom had assumed things were going reasonably well, and he hadn't considered that the campsite wasn't making money. If the only full-time employee wasn't getting paid, what hope did he have? Tom immediately felt guilty about worrying about himself instead of Ricky.

"Does Mum know you haven't been taking any wages?"

Ricky bowed his head slightly. "No, if she did, she'd know that things weren't going that well."

Tom looked toward Mike and whispered, "Shit, this isn't good."

Mike shook his head. "Look, let's go for a few pints, enjoy yourself and tomorrow. I'll have a look over the books before I go."

They took the short walk to the pub at the bottom of the road, and Mike still struggled to fully absorb the surroundings. Opposite the entrance to the campsite was a wooded area, and he could just hear the stream that presumably ran under the bridge and through the side of the pub. The pub looked even more appealing on foot, and he could now see the attractive beer garden to the rear of the property. Every inch of the building just exuded character.

Tom felt the pile of notes in his pocket, and knew that with nothing coming in, that pile would get smaller very quickly.

Ah, fuck it! he thought. *Something'll turn up!*

He pushed open the door of the pub and felt like a soldier returning from a glorious battle. He had already given thought to reasons why he'd returned from the city, as the last thing he wanted was for people to think he was a loser, coming home to live with his mum.

He prepared himself for a chorus of well-wishers quizzing him on life in the city and welcoming him back into the fold.

Mike quickly scanned the inside of the pub, and the charm was consistent with the outside appeal. The oak beams were prominent and had been decorated in places with tasteful brass ornaments. It was evident that the building had been heavily extended to incorporate a lounge area, which fell into the beer garden, but it had been done tastefully and didn't detract from the charm and feel of the building.

"It's a bit empty," observed Mike.

"Empty?" said Tom. "It's dead!"

Ricky looked puzzled. "It's the middle of the day. What did you expect?"

Tom felt a little deflated. He secretly imagined the locals rushing over and insisting on buying him a drink. The landlord's dog didn't even raise his head to acknowledge his triumphant return.

Tom looked over the bar but couldn't see anybody. After a few moments, he shouted, "Pope!" hoping to attract the landlord or at least someone to serve them. For once the landlord was not propped up at the bar sleeping. Mike looked around but couldn't see anybody.

After a short while a man dressed in poor quality grey trousers with a white shirt that had seen better days walked into the bar. The off-white shirt was unbuttoned at the bottom, which allowed a preview of the large gut that lay beneath. He had greasy hair and gave the impression of someone that needed a good wash. Mike assumed this was Pope, and was happy for him to serve beer, but wouldn't have been so keen if he was handling his food.

The man shuffled to the bar. "What'll you have, lads?"

Tom looked at Pope, trying to garner a glimpse of recognition, but nothing. Tom looked upset. "Are you taking the piss? Fifteen years I've been drinking in this place, and not even a bloody hello!"

A look of recollection appeared on Pope's face. "Shit, Tom, Ricky said you were coming back!" Pope raised a limp handshake over the bar. "Go on, first round on me, boys!"

Tom was pleased because Pope never gave out free beer, so despite the lack of a welcoming committee, this one gesture made him feel welcome.

Tom pointed toward Mike. "This is Mike, a friend from the city, and he's staying with us for a couple of days."

Pope pointed toward the large inglenook fireplace. "Get that fire going, boys and do you want some tits on the TV before it gets busy?"

Mike looked at Ricky, puzzled, as the offer was not one he was used to getting in a pub.

"Pope figured out how to wire up his computer to the TV, and always has the porn on when it's quiet," explained Ricky.

Tom looked equally confused. "No thanks. Maybe later, though!"

It wasn't cold, but the log fire added to the charm and feel of the place. Mike had a contented look on his face as he sat, drinking his pint, looking into the fireplace.

"You love all this, Mike?" asked Tom.

Mike didn't break his gaze from the fire. "I do. It's the way a pub should be — real ale, a log fire, and naked women on the TV. It's so much better than the cold, sterile pubs in the city. I could get used to this!"

"I watched that programme on the TV," said Mike. "You know, that one where a couple of gormless city dwellers jack it all in for a life in the country? I could never understand that, I mean why leave the city to live in the middle of nowhere? I've only just arrived and I get it, I can understand why people want to leave."

Tom laughed. "Is that because you're getting older, mate? One step closer to the pipe and slippers! Besides, all those people on those programmes have three million quid, one-bedroom box room they've sold to buy a nine-bedroom mansion in the country. Most of them are only young as well, bastards!"

"I just need a friend who'll let me pitch my tent once in a while," said Mike.

Pope walked over and placed a bowl of crisps on the table. "Your ex is working in here, Tom, three nights a week. I thought I'd better tell you now."

Tom grimaced. He knew he'd bump into Lou at some point, but she never drank in the pub, so he thought it would be a safe haven.

Pope looked at Tom sternly. "No trouble, Tom, she's a good worker."

Tom looked at Pope and raised his hand in acknowledgement. He had no intention of causing trouble. Quite the opposite. If he could permanently avoid her then he would do so.

Tom looked at Ricky. "That is all I bloody need. Did you know?"

Ricky nodded. "I knew it would piss you off, so I didn't tell you. Besides, move on! Jesus, how long has it been? Get over it!"

"He's right," said Mike. "You knew you'd bump into her at some point, so best getting that over and done with!"

Ricky reached over and threw more logs on the crackling fire. "She's put a load of weight on as well!"

Tom smiled. He wasn't sure why that made him happy, but if she wasn't as attractive, he figured it would make seeing her that much easier.

"Are you seeing anyone, Ricky?" asked Tom.

Ricky looked slowly around the empty pub. "No, there's nothing about. The only single girls are divorced women in their fifties or really ugly ones on their twenties."

Tom could sympathise, women and work were often a scarce commodity in a small village. Tom had been lucky with Lou, as he'd known her since they were children.

Mike finished his drink, and took the empty glasses to the bar to order another round of drinks. As he did, Tom leaned forward and whispered to Ricky, "So what's going on with Mum and Paul?"

"He's moved in with her! Pretty funny as they sat me down to talk me through it like I was a nine-year-old being introduced to my new stepdad. Paul's alright. He comes down here with me most weekends. Plus, Mum's happy."

Tom was pleased for his mum, and he knew Ricky was right. Paul was a good man, and he knew he would look after her.

"Did Mum tell you about the problem I had with Gypsies?"

Tom looked puzzled. "No, in what way?"

"I put that advert in the paper to try and get a few more bookings, you know, the one I told you about earlier. We didn't get any more bookings, but I woke up and there were about twenty caravans on the site. I assumed Mum must have booked them in and left them to it. Another ten turned up and there was shit all over the place, but they were pleasant enough, so I went to ask them to rein it in a little and get some cash off them. A couple paid me, but the rest told me to fuck off. It got a little bit heated, as a few of them Gypsies are big lads, and Christ they like to fight. Pope was having a nightmare with them as well. He liked the cash but they'd get pissed up and end up fighting with each other, so all the locals cleared off. I got a tractor-trailer off John from the top farm and put it on the entrance so at least that way no more caravans could get in. For the first couple of nights I got a load of speakers and played an ABBA CD full pelt so they couldn't get to sleep. They just smashed the speakers."

Mike stood listening, holding three pints. "Did you call the police?"

Ricky reached for his pint. "Yeah, they weren't interested, though. As long as they weren't causing trouble they were happy to leave them, and if they moved them on they knew they'd just be moving the problem further down the road. By this point, people who'd booked a pitch were turning up, taking one look at this lot and doing one. We were losing hundreds each week, so I got the muck spreader off John and covered all their caravans in shit."

Ricky drank his pint looking blankly at Tom, who shook his head. "And?"

"In hindsight, it wasn't a good idea to cover their caravans in shit, as they really love their caravans. Once they'd cleaned themselves up they smashed up the toilet block, which was one of the reasons I had to get it rebuilt. I turned the water off on them and even got a load of cockerels to see if the noise would get rid of them, but nothing worked. In the end I had to give them five-K to piss off."

Tom sat with his mouth wide open. "You had to pay them to go? Shit! No wonder you haven't been paid."

"There was nothing I could do."

Ricky looked over to Pope. "Tell them what those gypsies were like, Pope."

Pope walked toward them looking solemn. "Good drinkers, but it wasn't good, I thought they were going to kill Ricky when he covered them in shit!"

"So did I," smiled Ricky. "But it wasn't just me that was losing money. The whole village was. Most of the businesses, including Pope, threw some money into the fund to get rid of them."

"Shit, mate! You should have let me know."

Ricky looked Tom up and down. "Bugger-all you could have done, Tom, it's not like you were going to scare them away."

Ricky was twice the size of Tom, and knew how to throw a punch. Tom knew that if Ricky was worried then it must have been serious.

"Hang on," said Tom, "how much did the new toilet block and all the other stuff cost?"

Ricky paused for a moment. "About sixty-K all in."

Tom looked stunned. "Shit! Where did you get that from?"

"From Mum," said Ricky. "She tried to get a mortgage on the house, but as she's over sixty they wouldn't let her re-mortgage, so they gave her a loan."

"Secured on the house?" asked Mike.

"I think so. If she doesn't pay the loan, she loses the house."

Tom put his head in his hands. "Why didn't you tell me any of this?"

Ricky looked slightly annoyed. "Come on, Tom, what would you have actually done if I'd told you?"

Tom knew Ricky was right. What *would* he have done? He didn't have any money to help out.

The pub was getting busier, and Tom had seen a few familiar faces. People saw him and asked if he'd been on holiday, as they hadn't seen him for a while, but he chose not to correct them or let them know he'd been away for two years.

Ricky looked at Mike with a grimace on his face and gestured toward the door. Tom was standing at the bar and had not seen the door open.

Mike mouthed to Ricky, '*Is that Lou?*'

Ricky nodded. Mike was worried since Tom must have had six or seven pints by now, as they had each gone to the bar twice.

When Tom first moved to Manchester, he'd struggled with the breakup, and he still loved Lou. Carol and Mike were understanding, but Tom struggled to move on, and soon their sympathy waned. He had a habit of bringing Lou up in conversation when he was drunk, which was most of the time. Mike felt like he knew the girl due to the sheer amount he'd heard about her. He'd seen photographs of her, but it was strange to see her in the flesh. She was short, a similar height to Carol, but had darker hair, which was held back in a ponytail. Mike could see that she had a pretty face, but it wasn't a kind face. She had sharp features that made her look slightly solemn and, dare Mike think it, a little sinister.

Tom looked at Lou and he got that kicked-in-the-stomach feeling. He thought his legs were going to buckle. He had rehearsed this in his head dozens of times and wanted to keep to the script.

"Hi, Lou. You're looking well!" he said briefly, before taking his drinks and returning to the table. Lou smiled at Tom, but it was apparent that it was forced. He felt dejected as he approached his brother. "Ricky, you said she'd put weight on."

"She has!" said Ricky.

"I know! She's bloody pregnant!"

"Ah, I just thought she was fat."

Tom slumped in his chair, but was determined to be outwardly confident, as he didn't want Lou to know he was hurting. He reflected on what Ricky had said earlier, and he was right, it had been years since they'd been together, and he didn't like her. It still hurt him, but more because of the way they broke up, rather than the breakup itself.

Mike noticed a coach pull up in the car park. The passengers soon spilled into the pub. Pope wasn't keen on coach trips, as they were usually just a load of drunken kids dressed as Elvis. He cast a careful eye on the newcomers, but it was evident they'd been to a christening. There was a stately home about three miles up the road, which hosted a lot of weddings and christenings, but parking was difficult, so the owners would usually lie on a coach.

The pub was packed, and Mike was enjoying his introduction to the country life. Most city centre pubs wouldn't have this many customers in during the week unless there was a big football match on, and this was a small village pub in the middle of nowhere.

Tom didn't see much of Lou for the rest of the night, but when he did, he made a point of being polite and not overly talkative, as he didn't want to say anything that he'd regret in the morning.

The christening party had only stopped off for a quick drink but ended up staying for most of the night, much to the delight of Pope.

Tom looked at the christening party and turned to Ricky. "Ricky, how many camping huts have we got?"

Ricky paused, counting on his fingers. "Eight."

"And you can sleep how many in each hut? Four?"

"You can get six people in each one."

"And we have loads of sleeping bags and tents to rent out as well?"

Ricky nodded confidently. "Sure!"

Mike could hear raised voices coming from the christening party, and it was clear that people were starting to get irate. Pope had also noticed this, and came over to make sure nothing escalated.

The coach driver was stood in front of the party, who were now like a baying crowd. "They were in my pocket!" he pleaded.

It was difficult for the nervous driver to be heard over the volume of people shouting, but he eventually explained that he had come in to use the toilet, had a coke, and on his way back to the coach he realised his keys had gone.

A loud voice came from the crowd. "You must have a spare!"

The driver looked panic-stricken. "I do, but they're in the office! There's no way I can get a spare till the morning."

The same loud voice shouted, "What about taxis, and can you pay?"

Pope moved a little closer to avoid the situation getting out of control. "No chance for a taxi! You might get one or two to come out this way, but it's late and there's no way you'd get enough to take all of you home!"

Tom waded cautiously into the middle of the crowd, and the driver took refuge behind him. "Look, guys, it's a bit of a nightmare, but it sounds like you're stuck for the night till a spare turns up. We own the campsite up the road, and we've got camping pods, sleeping bags and everything you need!"

Mike was surprised at the generous offer, which had probably saved the driver from being hanged from the solid oak beams above them.

It wasn't ideal, but the christening party knew their options were limited, as did Tom. "Twenty pounds for the night, and the landlord will also throw on a load of chips."

Pope didn't mind, as he knew the punters would be drinking until they fell out of the bar.

The crowd gave a few discontented rumblings toward the driver, but there was little they could do. There was nowhere else they could stay and no way could they get home.

Tom counted up the cash and grabbed Ricky. "Eleven-hundred-and-twenty quid we've just made!"

Ricky looked shocked and unsure what exactly had just happened, but he did know that Tom had made more money on his first night than he had made all month. Ricky wasn't resentful; he just wished that Tom had come back earlier!

He looked at his brother and smiled. "You little beauty!"

Mike came over, looking slightly amused, and whispered to Tom, "So when are you giving him his keys back?"

Tom looked offended and paused before mouthing back. "In the morning should do it!" He gave directions to the christening party, and headed back to the campsite to get the huts ready and make sure everyone had sleeping bags.

Once there, he quickly emptied one of the huts that was being used as a temporary storage area. "Imagine how many hotel rooms we'd have to clean to make that sort of cash!"

"It's better on the grass," said Ricky. "We don't need to build a hut. People bring their own accommodation, and we charge them twelve quid a night to sleep on the floor. It's genius!"

Tom was starting to understand how much cash could be made from this place. He looked out at the vast swathe of grass — lit dimly by moonlight — and his mind worked in overdrive. "If we filled this place, we could pull in thousands each week!"

"Therein lies the problem," said Ricky. "It's good money, but you have to get the people through the gates!"

By the time the christening party settled, it was well after two a.m. and Mike and Tom were tired and drunk. They had given out all the camping huts, so they slept on the floor in Ricky's bedroom.

Tom didn't sleep much with the day's events playing over in his mind. He was glad to be back, and seeing Lou hadn't been as bad as he thought it would be. Instead, his mind was focused on the campsite and the realisation that they could make some serious money from it. Tom chuckled as he thought of Ricky covering an army of gypsies in shit and admired the way he had renovated the campsite.

Tom spent most of the night with a thought running through his head: *How do we fill a field in the middle of the country?*

Tom never slept well after drinking, and he woke early. He headed to the campsite to return the keys, and found the coach driver clambering under his coach.

Tom gently tapped the side of the coach. "Morning, driver! The landlord came by this morning, and thankfully, he found your keys."

The driver pulled himself up from the ground and dusted his company blazer. "Funny that, isn't it! I was in the pub twenty minutes ago, and the landlord hadn't seen them."

Tom could see from his expression that the driver wasn't stupid as he reached into his pocket and counted out one hundred pounds. He handed the folded notes to the driver. "This cover it?"

The driver counted the cash and smiled. "Sure! You could have got me bloody killed last night! Look, I am up this way two or three times a month taking wedding parties to Compton Hall. I have a bit of a habit of losing my keys."

Tom looked around and laughed as he handed the driver a note with his details on. "Funny that. I am quite good at finding them, eventually!"

The christening party headed toward the coach, with most of them looking like they'd had a heavy night. Tom personally greeted each customer, and handed them a flyer for the campsite. It was a beautiful sunny morning and he didn't want to miss the chance to promote the campsite to future customers.

He waved the coach off, and had a feeling he'd be hearing from the driver again. He took the short walk back to the house and walked into the kitchen where Mike and Ricky were enjoying a cup of tea.

Mike could see the coach pull away through the kitchen window. "So, he found his keys?"

Tom nodded as he pulled a large pile of notes from his pocket. "How nice does that look, Ricky! Here, stick this in your pocket and we can put the rest in the petty cash tin?" Ricky was delighted and gratefully placed the money in his pocket. Tom pulled out a piece of paper littered with numbers. "We need to fill this place with people other than the weekend punters. The cost of running this place is the same if we have five people or two hundred people. How do we fill a field in the middle of the country?"

Mike gave it some thought. "What about a beer festival?"

Tom stood up, excited. "I like it, come on, keep going, throw some more ideas at me!"

"What about a music gig? You know, like a festival?" suggested Ricky.

Tom looked at Ricky with a thoughtful expression. "That's brilliant! Genius!"

Ricky was unsure if Tom was being sarcastic, and a red flush came across his cheeks. Mike stood up and looked at the vast swathe of open field, and looked at Tom. "You know, that could work. It isn't a daft idea at all!"

Tom was excited, and started to pace the kitchen thinking about the options. He had no idea about the logistics but he liked the idea and he knew it could make money.

Tom walked over and slowly planted a firm kiss on his forehead. "Ricky, I don't know how, but we are putting on a music festival!"

Chapter Three

Lee!" screamed the voice down the phone.

The receptionist panicked, desperately searching through her records. "I'm sorry, sir, I cannot find a record. Could it be under any other name?"

"No! That's my name. Clint Lee! Put me through to Una Jacob, please!"

The petite receptionist was adamant. "Sir, I cannot find you on our files, so I cannot put you through to Una."

The man was clearly becoming more irate. "She's my bloody agent and has been for fifteen years!"

"Hold the line please, Clive!"

"Clint, not Clive!"

Clint paced around the room of his modern one-bedroom flat, cursing under his breath. In his hand, he was clutching a rolled-up ball of paper, squeezing it like some form of stress relief, becoming more annoyed by the monotone 'hold' music.

Emma, the trainee receptionist, reluctantly knocked on the matte-black office door. "I've got Clint Lee on the phone for you, Una."

Una looked up from her desk and scowled. "Tell him to fuck off. The guy's a fucking deadbeat!"

Emma took a deep breath and tried to project her voice. "But Una, he won't go. He's on the phone every day!"

Una reached into her filing cabinet and reached a long way back for the file marked Clint Lee and quickly scanned through it. Looking frustrated, she muttered, "Stick him through!" then took a deep breath and picked up the phone. "Clint Lee!"

Clint was surprised that he had finally got through. "Una, I've been calling you for a week. Hospital bloody radio!" he shouted, throwing the rolled-up contract he was squeezing in his hand.

"Three hundred pound a week, Clint, what more do you want from me? I'm not a bloody miracle worker!"

"But, Una, hospital radio? Come on!" said Clint.

"Clint, I won't lie to you. I don't like you! That said, I'm your agent, and if you make money, I make money. If you're making money for me, I like you, but you are not, and that is why I don't like you. It's harsh, but that's the way of the world. Because I don't like you, Clint, I can be honest with you. I won't bullshit you. You are a deadbeat!"

Clint was desperate to rip the phone out of the wall, but he needed Una. She was his only chance to get work. He looked dejected as he slumped into his chair dressed only in a pair of white underpants. His blond, floppy hair half-covered his face, but his scruffy facial hair was still visible.

"Look, Clint, I'm not out to hurt you, but you need to understand how the world works. You were in the charts fifteen years ago, and spent a few years in the musicals. You had a great ride. I'm amazed it lasted as long as it did. TV shows are churning out wannabe pop starts by the wagonload, and unfortunately most of them can sing better than you. You need to regroup and think about management, writing, whatever, but stop thinking you are going to get back on the stage. Trust me, honey, you ain't. And would it kill you to lose a few pounds? Cut out the booze, you look like shit."

Clint hadn't seen Una for months, but she was correct. He did look like shit.

Una softened her tone slightly. "Clint, I don't need to muck around with contracts like this, and I'm only doing this to get you on your feet. Are you interested or not?"

Clint continued pacing around his flat, desperate to tell her what to do with the job, but he needed the cash. He was behind with his rent, and his mobile was about to get cut off. He looked at the pile of unopened bills and reluctantly agreed. "No, but I'll do it!"

"You got it," said Una. "And get your fat ass on that treadmill!"

Clint clasped his head with both hands. "Fuck!"

A job offer like this would usually lead to him reaching for a bottle of whiskey, which served to numb the reality of the situation. Clint didn't have an ego, but he still had a modicum of self-respect, and when this was dinted, the usual remedy was to drown it out. He had made a concerted effort to clean up, and the harsh words of Una confirmed what he already knew.

Rather than empty the whiskey bottle, he continued to work on his autobiography. He was initially reluctant to write a book, but figured it was his way to make peace with those he had upset. People would surely be interested in his story, plus he needed the cash. However, he was well aware of minor celebrities putting out books as a last-ditch attempt to pull in some cash, and being viewed in this way had made him a little hesitant.

Writing down his innermost thoughts had been a painful experience, as it brought home to him what he'd wasted. His biggest cause of frustration was that he'd been sensible with his money. He didn't make a life-changing amount from his singing career, and whilst he was keen to enjoy the finer things, he put money to one side and had what would be considered a sizeable amount saved. He wasn't stupid, and had seen the majority of his peers enjoy fleeting success before drifting into obscurity. He cashed his chips in at the right time and leveraged his success to move into theatre. The money was good, and it was regular, and on the top shows he could be pulling in five thousand pounds a week.

When the show Clint was working on ended, he was keen to get back into the music business. However, he wasn't stupid. He knew he wasn't marketable, and that his best chance would be to move into music management. A former music producer had convinced him to invest in a recording studio, which was initially profitable, but soon began to haemorrhage cash. One of the acts that used the studio was a talented trio that had impressed him, and he suggested he manage them. He used his personal funds to promote them, but like the studio, this served only to further drain his cash. Soon enough, Clint realised that when the cash has gone, the phone stops ringing.

He looked around the small depressing flat he was currently renting. He could hear a phone ringing, which surprised him, as he thought that his phone had been cut off. He clambered under his sofa and found it surrounded by empty beer cans. He deliberately answered with confidence. "This is Clint."

He could scarcely hear a slight, reluctant voice on the other end of the phone. "Clint."

"This is him. Who's calling?"

"It's, um, it's Carol."

"Carol? Carol who?"

The quiet voice quickly became agitated. "Carol, you dick!"

He went quiet for a moment, racking his brains, trying to recognise the voice. "Holy shit! Carol, wow, I'm shocked, how are you?"

"I got your number from your sister. She said she's still pissed off with you."

Clint smiled for the first time in a long time. "It's great to hear from you, Carol, it really is!"

"Look, I honestly didn't want to phone you, and I'm only doing it reluctantly, as a friend could do with your help."

Clint listened intently. "Of course, if I can, I will. Let's face it, anything I could do for you would never make up for the way I treated you!"

"My friend Tom and his brother own a huge campsite in the country," she continued, "and they're looking at organising a music festival or something. You know, a few bands, a load of partygoers on the campsite for a few days, that sort of thing. The only problem is, they've never done it before, and thought you might want to get involved. As I said, I didn't want to phone you but they need help."

"That sounds good," said Clint. "Problem is, I'm doing a bit of TV work in the Far East at the moment, so no-can-do, I'm afraid."

Carol pulled the phone from her ear and gritted her teeth. "Bollocks! Your sister said I'd be lucky to get you on your mobile as you hadn't paid your bill for months. The boys are willing to pay if you can help them get this off the ground. Look, I couldn't care less if you help or not. I just said I would call you, but if you want to help, don't you even think about pissing them around. They're good friends!"

Clint could sense that Carol was annoyed. "Okay, you're right. The diary isn't exactly full at the moment. Are you still in the City?"

"Yes, the same house, near the hospital."

"You'll probably say no," said Clint, "but do you want to meet up this afternoon? We could talk more about this festival, and well, it would be great to see you again!"

Carol paused. It had taken all her courage to phone him in the first place. "Do you know Hugo's near Walpole Street? Three p.m. for a coffee?"

"Brilliant. See you then."

Clint was genuinely pleased to hear from Carol, and for once he had something to look forward to, something that would get him out of the confines of the flat. He hadn't had much cause to go outside, and he was in danger of becoming a recluse. Despite alienating those close to him, his family had remained loyal, particularly his sister, Pam. Pam had been friends with Carol, and she was the one who introduced her to Clint in the first place. When things deteriorated between them, Carol and Pam also drifted apart, although they occasionally kept in touch. Without Pam, Clint would have sunk without a trace.

As he rarely left the flat, he would often go for days without a shower or a shave, often wearing the same clothes for days on end, or just sitting in his underwear. Carol asking him for help had been a real boost for him, prompting him to take a shower.

Clint stood looking at himself in the mirror and smiled. It wasn't the same person looking back at him that he remembered from a few years ago. He felt better after a shave and even applied some aftershave. Clint looked through his sparse wardrobe and pulled out a smart pair of grey trousers, polished brown shoes and a Ted Baker shirt. Apart from the extra weight on his stomach, he looked smart, and felt motivated to lose a few extra pounds. He brushed his blond hair from his face, and was quite proud that he had retained a full head of hair.

The meeting point was about two miles from the flat, and he felt self-assured as he walked through the busy Manchester streets. He looked smart, and he looked like he deserved to be there.

He got to the coffee shop early, keen to get a good seat looking toward the door so he could see Carol come in. It was cosy, decorated with floral pictures and a dark oak floor. He looked around him, admiring the canvas prints on the wall, and soon became aware of a man near the door staring at him. This made him a little uneasy, but it wasn't unusual. People would often look at him, and knew they recognised him from somewhere, but weren't sure from where. Clint gave a brief smile, but did not hold his stare, in case the guy was just a head case.

The door opened, and Carol walked in. Clint smiled, and waved. It had been a few years since he'd last seen Carol, but she looked exactly the same with that pretty blonde bob and dark-rimmed glasses. She was dressed smartly in a black pencil skirt and pastel-coloured jumper. She smiled in return, but it was a deliberately cold smile. She had also made an effort, but a subtle one, as she was not trying to impress Clint; she just wanted him to know that she was doing okay for herself and life had gone on without him. For some bizarre women's logic, Carol didn't want to arrive first, so had been walking around for the last ten minutes to ensure she arrived fashionably late.

She walked towards Clint, and was a little surprised at his appearance. His boyish good looks had long since failed him, and he was carrying some extra weight. She thought this would make her happy, but it didn't; it made her feel a little sad.

She took off her coat and sat opposite Clint. "Your sister says you've been drinking too much."

Clint gestured toward the waitress. "White coffee, please."

"Same for me," asked Carol, smiling at the waitress.

Clint couldn't help but stare at Carol. "Are you still in advertising?"

She was reluctant to give away too much information to Clint. "No, I retrained as a nurse a few years ago."

Clint shuffled in his seat. He wasn't used to social occasions, and this was a difficult one. Looking down at the table, he mumbled, "I'm sorry, Carol. I was an asshole!"

She looked pleased to hear it, and deliberately delayed her response. "So, why were you an asshole?"

"Why? Shit, Carol, that's a question!"

Carol didn't respond, and stared at him with a look of content on her face.

Clint took his time and reflected on her question. It was one he'd considered a great deal whilst writing his book. "I thought I was a star. I shit on my friends, and worst, I shit on you. You get sucked into a false world, a place full of tossers designed to tickle your ego, and I liked it, or at least I thought I did. Carol, I wasn't always an asshole, it was only when I was singing. Once I stopped singing, my ego went, as did all the idiots. I wasn't always an asshole." He paused to gauge her reaction. "You look surprised."

"I am. I half expected you to sit here and tell me how it wasn't your problem, how you'd got in with the wrong crowd, blaming everyone except for Clint Lee."

Clint nodded. "I can understand why you'd think that. I started working in the theatre, and I loved it. I was surrounded by good people, I was pulling in good money, and I was looking after myself. Things went to shit, but that was only because of stupid investments and the show closing. Instead of getting my head down, I fell into a spiral of self-pity, which was stupid. I had job offers at the time as well, but once you start sinking, it's difficult to get back up. I mean it, though, Carol, I'm sorry. You were my rock, and I hurt you. Cheating on you was the thing I regret the most."

The waitress could see the emotion in Clint`s eyes, and cautiously placed the two drinks next to them.

"We had some good times, though? Didn't we?" said Clint, smiling. "Remember when I got my first big cheque?"

Carol nodded and broke a reluctant smile. "Edward Lewis, wasn't it?"

"Yes! The limousine was a Cadillac, it took me days to find one over here. You loved that film, *Pretty Woman?*"

"You took me to that beautiful hotel," said Carol. "You were lucky camera phones didn't exist back then, otherwise you would have been all over the Internet." She had long forgotten the good times in their relationship.

Clint took a sip from his coffee, desperately taking his time to drink it. "Anyway, what is this about a music festival?"

"My friend, Tom, and his brother are looking to put a festival on in a couple of months. I think they're struggling with the logistics, lights, stage, and all that sort of stuff. Tom knew that I know you, and asked if I'd give you a call to see if you could point them in the right direction?"

Clint responded without hesitation. "Yes, happy to help! It's been a while, but I still know a few people in the trade. What about acts? What are they thinking?"

"I don't know, to be honest," said Carol. "Knowing Tom, I don't think it's going to be a big-budget affair, but it's probably best if I put you in touch with them directly?" She looked at Clint with a look of suspicion. "You won't rip them off, will you?"

He looked genuinely hurt. "Jesus, Carol! I may have been an asshole, but I never ripped anyone off. I need to get my teeth into something, and this sounds like a bit of fun. Plus, I owe you, so hopefully this'll show you I'm not the person I was!"

He looked and sounded sincere. "Thanks, Clint. Look, I just need to be clear on one thing. Me and you, you know it'll never happen again, right? I know you probably weren't even thinking it, and if you weren't, I am sorry to bring it up. I just don't want it to be awkward!"

"Of course!" said Clint, trying desperately to hide his disappointment. He wasn't expecting Carol to come running into his arms, but since the phone call, he'd considered if it would be a possibility.

Carol finished her coffee and looked at her watch. "It's been good to see you again, Clint, and I mean that. I'll give Tom your number and ask him to give you a call?"

Clint stood up and helped Carol put her coat on. "Sure!" He leaned forward trying awkwardly to give Carol a hug. "It was great to see you, Vivian Ward!"

"Where's my limousine?" she asked, as she walked out of the coffee shop.

Clint sat down and finished his drink. He felt better than he had for a long time. It was only a brief meeting with Carol, but he felt like he was moving forward.

His thoughts turned toward the music festival, and this was something that excited him. He knew plenty of people in the industry, and had retained a lot of his contacts. From his experience, the most genuine people in the industry tended to be the hardest workers, such as the lighting crews, the stage people, and the roadies. They tended to be the ones that didn't pander to egos: if you were being a twat, they would tell you as much. Clint tried to recall if he had pissed off any of the people he would need to call. He was sure he hadn't, but it was a possibility. The first thing he needed to do was meet with Tom and his brother to scope out what they were looking to achieve. Where was the festival going to be, what sort of acts were they hoping to book, and most importantly, what sort of budget they were working to? Clint was helping as a favour to Carol, but he was sure he could somehow make some cash out of it as well.

Chapter Four

Ricky was howling, nearly doubled over on his knees. "I have just seen Chewbacca getting sucked off by Princess Leia!"

Tom looked over in disbelief, and sure enough could see a man in a costume holding onto the shoulders of Princess Leia.

"Use the Force!" shouted Tom.

Tom had been back at the campsite for six weeks, and they wanted to make as much money as they could before the summer months drew to an end. The site was busy with visitors, but he knew that to survive the long winter months they'd need cash in the bank.

Tom and Ricky had continued to work on the music festival idea, but knew they had to drum up some additional business. The campsite was going well, but it was just weekend campers, as it had always been. Tom had seen the coach driver on a couple more occasions, which pulled some extra cash in, but it wasn't enough. They needed more people, more of the time.

When Tom lived in Manchester, the local cinema had started a film club. They would pull out old classic films during the week when it was quiet, maybe stick some food on, and it seemed to be a great success. They were filling the place midweek.

Tom took a gamble and bought a second-hand outdoor cinema screen. It wasn't cheap, but he figured they could quickly get their cash back on it. As far as he was concerned, it wasn't enough for the punters to come and leave in quick bursts. He wanted them to stay for several days, so he could charge for admission and make extra money on camping fees.

Rather than a one-off film, he figured that if he got a whole series, such as Star Wars, people would stay for longer. He was right.

This was the first time he'd tried it, and he was staggered by how successful it had been. He'd sold the event from Sunday to Tuesday so it wouldn't impact on the usual weekend punters. He also put a few free adverts on Star Wars fan webpages, selling it as a Star Wars festival with prizes for the best costumes. He had even arranged for an actor from Star Wars, albeit a fairly obscure one, to turn up to mingle with the crowd.

Tom had charged fifty pound per person, which included a pitch for two nights. The punters had to bring their own tents, as they simply didn't have enough in the end. Tom sold nearly 250 tickets, and they could have taken a lot more. They sold lager by the caseload, which strictly speaking they weren't allowed to, but nobody was nearby to complain. Pope could have had cause to be upset, but his place was full during the day, so he was delighted. He thought the customers a little odd, but they were spending.

Allowing for expenses, and including beer sales, they would clear nearly £18,000 for three days' work. Ricky was staggered. He had been paid all of his back wages and there was plenty of cash going into the bank account. Their mum was also over the moon, as the site was her retirement income, and at last some money had started to filter through to her. Tom was keen to clear the loan, and the way things were progressing, that shouldn't take too long.

He had already thought of other themed nights: *Lord of the Rings, Star Trek...* Ricky had suggested a *Rocky* theme and they could get a boxing ring and invite the local amateurs down.

Tom was in his element, as he was finally doing something he was good at, and something he enjoyed. More importantly, for the first time, he was actually making money, *real* money!

Tom and Ricky stood at the back of the campsite, staring at the 250 people dimly-lit from the cinema screen. Around them stood rows of tents with rubbish placed lazily on the ground rather than in the bins provided. "Come on, Ricky, let's get this shit cleaned up," said Tom, jabbing at the floor with his extendable litter grabber. "It's tough at the top, hey Ricky!" He emptied a stinking bin into a large plastic bag.

Ricky smiled, picking up cans of discarded larger.

The crowd cheered in excitement and Tom looked over. "I never really got into Star Wars. I mean, it's okay, but to look at this lot, dressed up. It's a bit, well, you know."

"Fucked up?" suggested Ricky.

"Yes, a bit! Don't get me wrong. I like a good film, but to get dressed up... Maybe if you're an eight-year-old kid."

"I don't care what they get up to, as long as they pay their bill," said Ricky.

"Come on, Ricky, grab a chair. Let's have a beer and see what this rubbish is all about."

The rest of the night was trouble-free. The punters were just there to have a good time, and apart from a couple of trampled tents, there were no issues.

The coaches turned up fairly early the next day, and before long, the site had emptied, giving them the chance to clear the final bits of scattered rubbish and clean down the wooden camping huts.

"Did that really happen?" asked Tom, looking bemused.

Ricky looked at the empty campsite, and like Tom, could not believe the place was heaving the night before.

"It must have, because I have a load of cash in my pocket!" said Ricky.

Tom opened the door to one of the wooden huts and jumped back, startled. "Ricky, come here, quick!"

Ricky ran over to Tom and could quickly see a comatose Princess Leia lying on the floor, partially clothed.

Tom pointed to the apparent facial hair and whispered, "Princess Leia is a Prince!"

"Or a Queen!" laughed Ricky.

"You know what this means, Ricky?" said Tom. "Chewbacca must have turned to the Dark Side. Close that door, let him sleep it off. He can go when he's ready. The hut isn't booked."

Tom had now taken over the office, looking after the bookings and taking care of the business side of things, which pleased Ricky, who was happier taking care of the maintenance side of things. Tom could easily divert the office phone to his mobile, which meant that he and Ricky could get out whenever they wanted. He enjoyed his new job and the sense of responsibility it brought.

Pope was delighted at the renewed success the boys were having on the site. Most of the punters would come into the pub for an evening meal and a few drinks, and at certain times of the month he had to get extra staff on to cope with the influx of customers.

All of the shops in the village also benefited from the increased visitors. Tom knew that if he put an event on, he was covering the majority of the expense, which he was fine with, but he felt that other businesses that benefited should also throw some money into the budget. Nothing too excessive, just a few quid toward things like advertising budgets, flyers and infrastructure, such as signs, portable toilets and that sort of thing. So he asked around, and practically all of the business owners were glad to help out, as they knew that their businesses would also benefit. Pope was the most generous, as he was the one that benefited the most. If it had been a particularly good week, Ricky and Tom would find it difficult to spend their own cash in the pub, and Pope was like a new person, he had stopped drinking and sleeping on duty, and had lost a few pounds.

Pope was enjoying the increased business, but had been confused a few weeks earlier. A steady stream of customers were coming in, the majority carrying metal detectors. At first he didn't mention anything, but he couldn't figure out why there were so many of them.

"Where you staying, guys?" he asked them.

"At the campsite, just up the road," one of the group replied.

"Oh right! So what's with the metal detectors?"

The group looked a little confused. "We're looking for things, you know, in the ground," said the same person, trying not to sound sarcastic.

Pope could understand one or two people turning up, but there had been dozens over the previous few days. This stream of customers continued into the weekend, and by now, Pope had given up questioning it, and was just happy to serve them food and drink.

Tom had been in the pub with Ricky and was chatting with a few of the detectors who were staying on the campsite.

"Tom, what's going on with all these metal detectors?" asked Pope. "I've had loads of them in here but I don't know where they're coming from?"

Tom smiled, and asked Ricky to pass him over the magazine, which had a picture of a small child holding a handful of coins.

Pope put his glasses on and looked carefully at the picture. "That's Topper's young fella, isn't it?"

"Sure is!" said Tom. "He was in the top farm with his metal detector and found a load of medieval coins. Jammy little sod!"

"From the reign of Henry the Second, eleven-fifty-four to eleven-eighty-nine AD," said Ricky.

Tom looked at Ricky. "I'm impressed!"

"Jesus, what were they worth?" asked Pope.

"Tom bought them for three hundred pounds," replied Ricky. "So, about three hundred pounds!"

Pope looked blankly as Tom pretended to look at his watch. "Bloody hell, Pope, catch up. I thought Ricky was supposed to be the slow one!"

Pope shook his head. "You shady little shit! That is genius."

Tom looked proudly at Pope. "I saw Topper's boy in the village with his detector a few days ago. He told me he'd found a couple of keys, but nothing exciting, so I bought a few coins off the internet, which wasn't cheap. I saw Topper's lad a couple of days later and asked, well, suggested that he try up the top field, as I remembered from school there'd been a fort, or something there. After about an hour or so, bingo! Topper's boy has found treasure, so he's over the moon."

"Tom was kind enough to let the detectors societies know," added Ricky. "So they sent up one of their reporters, who did a full-page spread. It got into the papers as well!"

"Ha, brilliant, I love it!" said Pope. "It's been like a gold rush around here lately."

"Yeah, it was a bit of a gamble," said Tom. "We could have been three hundred quid out of pocket, but we must have had a couple of hundred people staying over, so it turned out pretty good. Keep it from Topper, though, eh? His boy is like a local hero at school."

"I'm glad he went for this idea to get the customers in," said Ricky. "The other option was a Nessie-style sighting up at the reservoir!"

"Keep that one to yourself, Ricky! We might be doing that one next year."

Tom's phone rang, disturbing the final clean-up from the *Star Wars* showing. Tom answered, and mouthed to Ricky, '*It's Clint Lee!*'

"Clint, good to hear from you. Thank you for calling."

"No problem. Carol said you were looking at running a festival?"

With all the enthusiasm of a child at Christmas, Tom told Clint about the campsite and the events that they had run over the past few weeks. He'd been a little sceptical about speaking with Clint, particularly as Carol had not spoken about him in glowing terms, but Tom needed help if they were to proceed with the music festival, and Clint was potentially the ideal person.

"It sounds great said," said Clint. "And to be honest, what you want to do is definitely achievable, but it comes down to budget, and what you're willing to spend."

"I'm thinking of doing something with a bit of an eighties theme. Get a stage and a few bands, burger stalls, a Ferris wheel, fairground stalls, that sort of thing. What do you think?"

"As I say, it is definitely doable. Your problem is going to be the cost of the bands. A lot of the bigger groups will be booked up months in advance, and you'd probably be looking at twenty to forty K for each band. If you want to go for a festival style over a couple of days, you would need a few bands to pull the crowds in. The stage could be anything from ten to thirty K, and then you have advertising costs, insurance, the list just goes on!"

Tom looked dejected as he quickly wrote down the figures. "Shit. We could be looking at hundreds of thousands?"

"Easily," replied Clint. "And I know from first-hand experience how quickly you can lose your cash in this industry. It is full of shitbags, and I used to be one! Seriously, though, Tom, think about it. Carol says your campsite's big, but you would need a lot of people to make it work on those figures. Also, think about what happens if it rains, or what happens if the lead singer gets ill. It could be a major risk for you. I am out your way in a few days, should I give you a ring and I can drop by and have a chat in greater detail?"

"Yeah, that would be great. Listen, Clint, I really do appreciate your help on this. See you soon."

Tom wasn't stupid and knew it would be expensive to do, but he had definitely underestimated the costs. He ran some rough calculations, and from a risk-reward perspective, there was no way it would work. He would need about eight to ten thousand punters, and for a small music festival in the middle of nowhere, he knew that was never going to happen.

Ricky stuck his head around the office door. "Any good?"

"Not really. Big bucks… we could be looking at a couple of hundred!"

"Thousand?" said Ricky.

"Yeah. It was a good idea, but it's back to the drawing board."

Tom was disappointed, as he liked the idea of putting on a music festival, but on those figures it would have been suicidal to risk any money they'd earned on such a high-risk event.

"Anyway, forget that for now," he said. "I have had another idea!"

He gestured Ricky to follow him, and they walked to the top end of the field near to the overflow area.

"You did most of the building work for the new toilet block, Ricky. What do you think about knocking up a couple of cabins for us to live in? I'm living in a small hut and you're living up with Mum, which is not ideal."

"Yeah, definitely!" said Ricky without hesitation.

Ricky paced the area, marking out where he could put a couple of log cabins. There was plenty of room to put two good-sized cabins next to each other without impacting on the available space for people camping.

Tom could see the glimmer in Ricky's eyes, and it was obvious it was something he was eager to do. "You look into that, Ricky, scope how much it would cost, and see if we can swing it. See if we can do it without needing planning permission, as that'll add months and cost a fortune!"

Tom left Ricky, playing with what looked like an imaginary Lego set. Ricky didn't have any formal building qualifications, but Tom could see the standard of his work on the shower block. There was potentially enough money in the budget to get tradesmen in where required. Tom had been thinking about making his move permanent, but he knew that a grown man could not live in a camping hut full-time. There was no plumbing in the hut, so he had to walk across the field every time he needed the toilet or a shower. He'd looked into the options of buying something in the village, but he'd have no chance, as the prices were far out of his reach. House prices had always been high, but in the last few years they'd soared. This was great news for people who owned property and were looking to move out of the village, but for those looking to buy in the village it was unrealistic. Children grew up in the village and when they were looking to buy their first home, often the only option was to leave the village or continue to live with their parents. Ricky had wanted to move out of the house years ago, but like many, fell into the trap of rising house prices. Building a couple of low-cost cabins on the land they already owned was the ideal option. Tom was looking forward to getting stuck into a project the two of them could work on. Plus he knew his mum would be pleased to get the house back.

Winter had finally started to draw in, and the campsite was empty. Lou had a baby boy, and Tom was pleased for her, always making a point of catching up with her when he saw her in the village, but only when she wasn't with Pete. Tom didn't hold any bitterness; he simply didn't like the guy, which was unusual for Tom, who could get on with anybody.

He kept his promise and stayed in close contact with Mike and Carol, who would usually come out and stay on the site every couple of weekends. It was a bit more difficult for Carol due to working shift patterns at the hospital, but Tom really enjoyed their visits, and would light the campfire and arrange a few drinks under the stars, usually inviting their mum and Paul, Pope from the pub and a few other friends from the village. He was always pleased to see them both but felt flat when they left, especially Carol.

Tom continued to be impressed by Ricky, and he often felt guilty that he thought of Ricky as a little slow, and that he hadn't defended him when others had said the same. Ricky had never taken offence, and as he was solidly built, people only tended to say it light-heartedly rather than with malice. Ricky had certain skills, which were best suited to an outdoor, manual person. In a structured environment, he struggled, and would appear slow and cumbersome. It was just a case of the right man for the right job. Ricky had been working nonstop on the new log cabins, and everyone, especially his mum, was immensely proud of what he had achieved. Apart from a few specialist trades, Ricky had built the bulk of the cabins himself, and was confident of finishing before the harsh winter arrived. They were relatively cheap to build, and as Ricky had provided the majority of the labour, he was confident of completing them well within the modest budget.

Tom sat in the office, desperately thinking of ways to make money. He looked out of the window and the grass was empty. The weather had turned, which he knew would happen, but it didn't stop him feeling depressed as he looked at the lonely campsite.

His misery was interrupted when his phone rang. He could see Carol's name appear on the display. This always brought a smile to his face.

Carol's voice was sombre. "Tom?"

He could hear the stress in her voice, and panicked. "Yes, what's up? Are you okay?"

Carol was clearly upset, and her voice was breaking. "Tom, it's Mike. He's in hospital and he's in a bad way."

Tom went quiet for a moment, and slowly lowered himself into his seat. "What happened? Will he be okay?"

"They think he's got a fractured skull, broken ribs and fractures in his arm. His family are with him now. Tom, I was working when they brought in him. I didn't recognise him."

Tom could hear her sobbing on the phone. He felt helpless, and desperately wanted to take her in his arms. "Shit. Look, where are you now? At home?"

"Yes. Work told me to come home. I stayed with Mike until his family got there. He's a mess!"

Tom frantically looked at his watch. "Okay, I'm coming. If I leave now I should be there by lunch!"

"Okay," said Carol. "But, Tom, please drive carefully."

Tom ran over to Ricky and explained what had happened to Mike. Ricky was keen to go with Tom, but they needed somebody to stay and look after the office. Tom still didn't have a car, as he had no need for one. Luckily, his mum was at the house and agreed to lend him hers.

Tom started the familiar journey into the city, but this time it was with a gut-wrenching feeling. He was conscious that he was driving too fast, and Carol's warning about driving too quickly echoed in his head. He took a deep breath to compose himself. It was over a hundred miles into the city, and he wanted to make sure he got there in one piece.

What the hell happened to him? He became aware that he had not asked Carol what had caused these injuries. *Had he been in a car crash? Fallen down the stairs?* Tom couldn't help but think the worst.

He thought about his school days with Mike, and it brought a welcome smile. Mike excelled at school, and was able to balance being intelligent with being popular. Tom was just popular, but had a desire to be intelligent.

Tom and Mike formed an unofficial partnership at school catering for the growing demand for parties. Word would spread that a house was available, and Tom and Mike would start the process of convincing the liberated child that a house party was a good idea. They would make all of the arrangements, and for their services they would sell tickets to the party. The reason their parties were such a success was that they budgeted for security and cleaning. The security would ensure only those with tickets could get in, and once in they would ensure that everyone behaved. Cleaners would then return the house to the original state.

After paying the cleaners and security, Tom and Mike would usually clear a hundred quid each, which was a sizeable sum for a couple of teenagers. The host would usually get a percentage of the door money, and more importantly gain kudos within their peers for throwing a party. It was a solution that worked, as they knew kids would always have a party, so why not do it in a controlled environment?

Unfortunately, the demand far outweighed the supply of houses available, so this source of income was brought to a natural conclusion.

The pair continued their partnership, acting as the unofficial school bookmakers, taking bets that older friends would then place with the official bookies. These were the days before mobile gambling was available, and business was booming. Tom and Mike would never take a financial risk, but would take a percentage of the amount wagered, usually ten percent, with the remaining ninety percent placed as the wager.

To increase their earnings, they would occasionally take the bet on themselves rather than place it with the official bookies. This meant that if the bet wasn't a winner, they would get to keep the entire stake, but if the bet won, they would have to pay out of their own pockets.

Another difficulty came in ensuring the older friends were trustworthy and would actually hand over the proceeds of a winning bet. Either way, Tom and Mike would have to pay regardless of whether they received the money. They made good money from the gambling business, but there were too many variables that were out of their control. They made plans to go into business when they left school, but Tom was realistic: he knew Mike would be going to university, whereas he had no intention of extending his education.

Tom often wondered what they would have done had Mike not gone to university. Would they have gone into business? Would they have been a success?

The drive went quickly, and Tom pulled up outside Carol's house and quickly ran to the door. He thought about using his front door key, but chose to ring the bell. Carol opened the door and looked tired and drained. She gestured at Tom to come in, and instantly gave him a warm, welcoming cuddle as Tom brushed her hair off her face and kissed her on the cheek.

Composing herself, she said, "He's a mess, Tom, and I didn't recognise him."

Tom was unsure of the chain of events. "Were you working?"

"Yes, I was with him for about five minutes before I saw his name on the notes. My legs buckled and I felt physically ill. The police then came in to ask me a few questions, and asked me for his next of kin, just in case. I gave them his family's contact details. I should have phoned them, Tom, not left it to people that didn't know him."

Tom tried to reassure her. "You did the right thing! Is his family with him now?"

"They got there before I left. It was awful, Tom, his poor mum," sobbed Carol.

"Shit, will he be okay?"

"It's too early to tell. He was barely conscious when I left. I wanted to stay, but his family arrived. I said I would come back when you arrived if that's okay?"

"Yes, of course. Have you eaten, are you hungry?"

Carol moved toward the door. "No, let's just grab a sandwich on the way." She turned to look at Tom. "Thanks for coming so quickly!"

The tired look was now replaced with one of relief, as Carol linked his arm. He turned and kissed her gently on the cheek. "Do they know what actually happened?" he asked.

"I don't have all the information, only a bit the policeman said when he was admitted. He was cycling to work, and a car driver found him lying in the road. They called an ambulance and brought him in."

Tom felt angry. "A hit and run?"

"I don't think they know. The police are looking into it."

"Mike's tough. He'll be fine."

Carol smiled. "No he isn't, he's soft as shite. But I know what you mean!"

Tom was pleased to see Carol smiling, and he didn't like to see her upset. He was distracted by a familiar voice on the radio, and reached to turn the volume up. "Ha! Is that Clint?"

Carol nodded. "Have you not heard his song on that annoying advert?"

Tom shrugged his shoulders.

"It's on some daytime advert, one of those stupid compensation ones. Unfortunately, the next generation appear to like the song. He was telling me there's talk of releasing the song again, and who knows, maybe a comeback tour."

"A comeback. Shit, did Mike know? Maybe he deliberately rode into a bus."

They laughed, and Carol gave him a friendly slap on the leg.

Tom parked in the hospital and now felt a sickening feeling return. Carol could see the concern in his face, and gently resumed linking his arm.

He took a deep breath and walked into the all-too-familiar hospital. The last time he'd been here was when his father had died.

They were quiet as they walked onto the ward, and Carol was the first to see Pauline, Mike's mum. Carol walked over to her and gave her a big hug. "How is he?"

"Conscious," Pauline said, looking relieved. "He is still in a bad way, but they're confident that he'll pull through, thank god!"

Carol took an intake of breath. "You remember Tom?"

Tom moved toward her and gave her a hug. "Of course I do. Thank you for coming. You have both been such good friends to Mike. It is great to see you both, and Carol, thank you for looking after him today!"

Pauline wiped a tear away from her face. "I thought we were going to lose him when I first saw him."

Carol moved toward her and put an arm around her shoulder.

Tom waited a moment. "Do you mind if we see him?"

Pauline nodded, and moved them toward the private room opposite. Tom gave a gentle knock and entered the room with trepidation.

The room was bright, and Tom could immediately see Mike surrounded by tubes, with a nurse taking his blood pressure. Even from the other side of the room, Tom could see that Mike was a mess. He walked closer, and Mike briefly looked over to him and attempted to smile, but it came across as more of a grimace.

The nurse smiled at Tom. "Ten minutes, as he needs to get some rest."

Tom nodded and smiled. The nurse left the room and he stood at the foot of Mike's bed, consciously trying not to look shocked at his appearance, but Tom had known Mike for too long and couldn't hide his true feeling. Mike looked swollen and bruised and Tom could understand why Carol had been so concerned.

"My god, Mike, you look like shit. Seriously. I thought I was in the wrong room."

Despite the swelling, Mike was able to talk, although more in a hushed tone. Tom couldn't hear what he was saying, and moved a little closer. Still unable to hear, Tom virtually had his head on Mike's chest as he mouthed the words, 'piss off.' Tom could have cried, and he was never happier to hear someone swear at him.

He felt instantly relieved, and despite the outward appearance, Mike was in a better state than he thought he would be.

Tom reached into a bag and pulled out a newspaper and the obligatory puzzle book bought from the hospital shop. "Before your mum comes in, there's another little magazine in the newspaper I picked up from the garage," said Tom with a wink. "It should move the swelling elsewhere!" he added.

Mike could actually talk louder than he'd let on, and Tom was pleased to hear his voice. "I bet that magazine is well used!"

Tom looked puzzled. "Mate, what happened to you? Did you just crash?"

Mike paused for a moment, recalling the crash. "No! Someone hit me. I was just riding and I saw a van from the corner of my eye, and the next thing I know, I am waking up in this place. The police were in before because the driver didn't stop. I told them I couldn't give them any information, so they're hoping someone saw the crash, or maybe it was caught on CCTV."

"Bastards!" said Tom. "There are cameras everywhere, mate, they will catch him. Carol is outside talking to your mum. She was on duty when you came in, so was quite upset. She phoned me and said she didn't even recognise you when you came in!"

"Mum said. It must have been a bit of a shock for her."

There was a gentle knock on the door, and Carol appeared with a beaming, caring smile that came so naturally.

"Only me," she said as she walked over and reached for Mike's hand. "God, you look a bit better now than you did before."

She was obviously being polite, since Mike still looked swollen, but at least he was now conscious and talking.

"Thanks, Carol!" said Mike. "In fact, thank you to you both for being here. Carol, I hope I didn't scare you too much?"

"You did a bit, mate, but a few days in here and you'll be back on your feet."

"I broke my bloody glasses as well," said Mike.

"Better than your neck, though. I'll bring your contact lenses in tomorrow."

"Anyway, your sister has just turned up, and is outside with your mum," said Carol, looking at Tom. "We'll go, so you can see them. We'll come back and see you in the morning?"

"Sure," said Tom. "I'll stay over, and we can come see you tomorrow."

"Enjoy your magazine!" said Carol, who smiled and then looked knowingly at Mike and Tom.

Carol and Tom said goodbye to Mike and his family, and headed to the car park. Tom felt like a huge weight had been lifted, and walked a little easier. Tom put his arm around Carol. "You okay?"

"Better now, thanks. And thanks for getting here so quickly. I felt a bit lost on my own."

"When you mentioned the fractured skull, I thought the worst," said Tom. "It's a cliché, but stuff like this really does make you realise how quickly things can change!"

Carol nodded. "So are you going to stay over tonight? Your room is now full of junk, I'm afraid, but I'm sure Mike wouldn't mind you using his room."

"Great. Ricky is looking after things, so I don't need to rush back. How about I take you out for a meal and a couple of drinks?"

"Just a couple of drinks? Do you think I'm a cheap date," said Carol with a laugh.

Tom dropped Carol off at the house before going into town to buy supplies for his impromptu sleepover. He'd not been away from the city for long, but was shocked by how busy it was. *Give me the countryside!* he thought to himself. He negotiated his way around the shops and thought about where to take Carol for a meal. Previously he would have settled for a takeaway, but he was now pulling in fairly decent money, and wanted to take her out for a nice meal. He was conscious that he was thinking about her more than he had for a while. That smile made him feel warm inside, and seeing her upset made him realise how much he cared for her. He hadn't considered if she had a boyfriend, and panicked when he considered it a possibility.

He pushed his way through the crowds as he felt a hand grab him firmly on the shoulder. He turned around, instinctively raising his hands and taking a step back. "Larry!"

Tom lowered his hands and immediately realised how ill-prepared he would have been in an attack situation.

Larry smiled. "Jesus, Tom, you're a bit jumpy. It must be all that country air!"

Tom caught his breath. "Larry, great to see you! I was going to pop in and say hello, but I wasn't sure if you'd be in."

Larry walked closer to Tom, a little closer than he was comfortable with. "I'm not happy with you, Tom!"

Tom panicked and mumbled his words. "If it's about the text, I was going to come and tell you I was going, Larry. Did you get my text? I hope you got my text!"

Larry smiled, which instantly relieved the tension. "I got the text, son. A phone call would have been better, but whatever. The punters miss you, Tom, and I miss you. Are you coming back? There is always a job for you."

"Larry, that means a lot, it really does," said Tom, "but I'm enjoying the change. I miss the old job, of course! You are looking well, Larry!"

Larry looked immaculate in his grey, tailored suit, as he always did, with his open-necked white shirt revealing an elegant gold chain. His thin, greying hair was slicked back, and at first glance, Larry appeared like any other ageing businessman in the city. But there was something in the face that set him apart, his piercing eyes or maybe his weathered nose. Either way, Tom knew that Larry commanded a quiet respect.

The old man put his firm hand on Tom's back. "Come on, let's go for a coffee."

Tom was eager to get back to Carol, and wanted to politely decline, but Larry had a naturally persuasive way about him, and Tom thought it better to oblige.

It was a short walk to the office where Tom worked, and Larry took him into the office at the rear of the shop. Tom was pleased to be back in the shop, and smiled as he saw the same old locals sat on the same stools; it was as though he hadn't left.

Larry sat down in a large green leather seat, and pulled out two glasses and a bottle of whiskey from his desk.

"I thought we were going for a coffee?" said Tom.

"Whiskey, coffee, it's all good."

Larry was thoughtful, and didn't waste words, which added to his imposing persona. "So you're running a campsite. Bit boring?"

Tom reached for his whiskey. It had been a tough day, and he was grateful for something stronger than coffee. "At times, Larry, but it's rewarding, and when it's busy the money is good, really good. I just need to get a few more punters through the door when it's quiet, a bit like any business I suppose."

One thing Larry could respect was money, and his interest perked up a little more as Tom told him about the events they had organised. Although it was in the early stages, Tom brought up the idea for the music festival.

Larry leaned in his chair. "You need money?"

Tom was caught off guard. "Money?"

"I like you, Tom, I always did. If you need money to make this happen, look at it as an investment. Come and see me, okay?"

Tom was flattered. Larry wasn't stupid, and wouldn't consider investing in something unless he thought it had a chance of making money. But Tom also knew that Larry was a lovely bloke when you didn't owe him money.

Larry could see that Tom was on the back foot. "Don't decide now, Tom, just think about it!"

Tom nodded his head. "I will, Larry. It means a lot. Thank you! You need to come and spend the weekend on the site, have a look around."

Larry smiled. "Do you think I get a tan like this from the beautiful British countryside?"

"Fair point, Larry, but the offer is always there if you fancy a day out in the country. By the way, out of interest, where would I take a lady for something to eat? You know something special?"

"Barkers," said Larry. "Tell them I sent you."

Tom finished the remnants of his whiskey. "Thanks, I'll check it out. I need to get going Larry, but it's been great to see you. My friend is in hospital and I said I'd get a couple of things for him."

Larry stood up and walked toward the door. "Nothing serious, I hope?"

Tom followed Larry into the main shop. "He's on the mend Larry. Just a bit of a shock for everyone."

As they walked through the main shop, a couple of the regular customers smiled and acknowledged Tom. Larry gave Tom a firm hug. "I mean it, Tom. If it doesn't work out for you, give me a call?"

Tom was genuinely impressed with how sincere Larry was. "I will! I mean it, and if you can, it would be great if you pay us a visit?"

Tom looked at his watch. He had been a lot longer than he thought. He quickly walked back to Carol's house as he phoned the restaurant and made a reservation at Barkers. He knew that if Larry recommended it, it must be good.

There was no answer when he arrived back at the house, but he soon realised from the volume of the stereo that Carol was getting changed. He smiled as he heard the Belinda Carlisle CD that he almost knew word for word from his time living there.

He needed to borrow a shirt, and was sure that Mike wouldn't mind, as he carefully flicked through his array of shirts. He poured Carol a glass of white wine, and shouted up to her so she didn't get a fright. As she walked into the front room, Tom was a little stunned. "Wow, you look amazing."

"Why, thank you," replied Carol taking a sip from her glass.

She looked Tom up and down. "You look and smell like Mike!"

Tom was only used to seeing Carol in her uniform or casual clothes, and rarely had he seen her dressed up. Her tight black dress revealed her cleavage and more of her legs than Tom had seen before. He desperately tried to avoid staring, but couldn't help himself, something that had not gone unnoticed by Carol.

"So where are we going?"

"The Chinese on the main street," said Tom.

Carol looked a little disappointed and didn't try to hide it.

Tom smiled. "Would I take you to Chinese looking like that? We're going to Barkers in town. It comes highly recommended!"

Carol looked relieved. "Sounds classy, like me!"

Tom heard the taxi pulling up outside, and drank the rest of his wine. "Our carriage awaits, m'lady!"

It was a short drive to the restaurant, and when they arrived it looked elegant with imposing columns flanking the entrance doorway, and vast swathes of glass providing a preview of the sumptuous interior.

"I could get used to this! A little better than a takeaway!" said Carol.

The maître d' provided a warm welcome and escorted them to a cosy table at the rear of the restaurant.

Tom looked through the menu. "I don't know why I bother looking! Fillet steak medium rare with chips every time! Let me guess, fish for you?"

Carol shook her head and continued scrutinising the menu. "I'm not as predictable as you!"

The light of the candle gave Carol a warm glow, her face half obscured by the menu. Tom pretended to read the rear of the menu, using the opportunity to appreciate how pretty Carol looked. "Do you always chew your lip when you're thinking?" he asked.

"Yes, it makes me look intelligent!"

"It's cute."

Carol purposefully placed the menu on the table. "Fish, by any chance?" asked Tom.

Carol smiled. "Yes! Like you, I am boring and predictable. It is part of my charm."

"Don't forget cute!" said Tom.

He was aware that his last comment had made him blush, and was hopeful that the romantic light levels had hidden the fact. He was entering uncharted waters, and was unsure if Carol actually had any feelings for him.

He desperately scanned her face, hoping for a signal that he'd not pushed things too far. She paused for a moment before playfully chewing her lip again before blowing a pretend kiss.

"Red or white wine?" asked Tom.

"Red, please."

Rather than pretend he was an aficionado of the wine list, Tom took the safe option and ordered a bottle of house red. Then he poured two generous glasses. "To Mike and a speedy recovery. And the loan of this awful shirt!"

"Don't forget the bad aftershave!"

Tom pretended to throw his napkin at her. "Do you think he'll be okay? I mean really okay?"

"I do! He's talking, and the injuries aren't as bad as first thought. I feel better now than when I first saw him. I thought he was done for today, I really did." She took a sip of her wine, then wiped her lips with a napkin. "Anyway, farmer boy! Tell me about life in the country. Is it full of frisky little milkmaids in dungarees?"

Tom laughed. "What countryside have you been to? You've seen my village. It isn't exactly teeming with available ladies. The available ones have either been with Ricky, have webbed feet, or I'm already related to them!"

"I thought that being related didn't bother you *country* folk!"

Tom enjoyed seeing Carol smile, and he enjoyed her company. As he looked across the table, he was desperate to know if she had any feelings for him. She was one of his closest friends, and he didn't want to risk that friendship by saying something stupid.

"Next time you come out, I'll have a spare room for you. Ricky has nearly finished our log cabins!"

"What, so no more living in a shed?"

"I know! I won't need to walk across a field to go for a pee. I'm moving up in the world. Things are going well, though. Work is busy, and I finally got some money coming in!"

"Just as well, otherwise we'd be doing the dishes all week in this place. How are things going with you and Lou? Was it awkward?"

"No. Well yes, a bit," said Tom. "It was when I first got there, but I just stayed out of her way. Seeing she was pregnant wasn't good, but it helped, as it made me draw a line under it, a bit of closure!"

Carol tilted her head to one side and gave a warm smile. "At least you're moving forward now! So what do you do with a campsite in the winter? It must get a bit quiet?"

"Dead, more like! I've got a few ideas to get people in, though — some good and some not so good. I'm going to put on more of those film nights, which went quite well. And we had an enquiry from an astrological society. Apparently the village is great for looking at the sky. No light pollution. So people turn up with their telescopes and stay for a couple of days. Its easy money, I just need to get more of these people through the door."

The waiter carefully placed the meals on the table, and gracefully refilled the wine glasses.

Carol admired her meal. "I like being predictable. This looks good."

"It does, but the portion is a bit small," said Tom.

"I thought you would be used to a small portion!" said Carol with a chuckle.

Tom smiled. "You're blushing!"

Despite the portion size, the food looked stunning. Tom eagerly cut into his steak, which was cooked to perfection, as he gave a look of appreciation to Carol. "So, will you come out when the cabin is finished?"

"That depends," said Carol. "Are there any restaurants like this place? You've created a monster, a culinary monster!"

"Not quite, but Pope does a mean scampi!" Tom looked at Carol enjoying her meal, and she looked at home amongst the elegant backdrop. "Have you ever sworn?"

Carol looked up with a puzzled expression. "What? That's a strange question, you weirdo."

"I'm serious. I don't think I've ever heard you swear. In fact, I don't think I have ever heard you say a bad word about anyone."

"Would you like me to?" asked Carol.

"No, it's sweet. I like it."

"Cute and sweet in the same night, Tom! Are you getting softer in your old age, or is the red wine kicking in?"

Tom paused for a moment. "Both, I think? Or I've been surrounded by too many girls with six fingers for too long!" As she laughed, he smiled at her. "Do you remember the first time we met?"

She looked up and thought for a moment. "No, I honestly don't."

"Memorable, then!"

"Why do you?"

"Not really, although I do remember you turning up to Kyle Lafferty's party dressed as Minnie Mouse!"

"They told me it was a fancy-dress party! I do remember you and Mike selling tickets to those parties, though. I thought you were pretty cool, as I remember. Maybe even groovy? I'm not sure what a fourteen-year-old girl would have said?"

Tom laughed. "Groovy! I will go with that one. I do remember asking you to the sixth form prom, and you said no. It had taken me weeks to pluck the courage up to ask you, as well."

Carol was shocked. "Ah, you lying little monkey! I know for a fact you asked Debbie Turner and Lisa Ryan to go with you before me, because I was stood next to them when you asked them! You only asked me when they'd said no, and by the way, Casanova, do you remember how you asked me?"

Tom cringed. "No, but I'm guessing it wasn't good?"

"You are correct! But if you don't remember, I'm not telling you!"

Tom shuffled in his seat slightly, looking a little flustered. "Yeah, but that's all in the past. What about that fish!"

Carol leant back in her seat. "That meal was stunning!"

He gently pushed the menu toward Carol. "It was. Room for dessert as well?"

"No chance! Oh, okay then, if we're doing the dishes we may as well get our money's worth!"

The waiter, who was well versed in the turmoil of dessert guilt, arrived to take the order and poured the remains of the wine bottle.

"Can I fetch you another bottle as well, sir?"

Tom looked at Carol for approval, and took her raised eyebrow as a sign of acceptance. "Yes, please."

"Very good, sir"

"You're going to get me drunk!" Carol said.

Tom paused for a moment. He really liked Carol, but the last thing he wanted to do was have any decisions influenced by drink. "Sorry, two coffees instead of the wine." Carol looked surprised and slightly relieved. "I don't want to forget a really nice evening by getting steaming on wine," he continued. "Plus I know you start crying when you get too drunk!"

Carol pretended to be offended. "I do *not!* Okay, maybe once in a while. Anyway, have you cut down on the drink?"

"I still drink, but nowhere near as much. It was getting a bit heavy when I was in the city, but that was more about boredom, to be honest. Don't get me wrong, I still like a drink. Just not as much. I haven't had a bet for weeks either. I guess country life cures all sins!"

"You had enough of them!" She had a broad grin as the waiter returned and placed the dessert on the table. She leaned over the table and cut a small piece of Tom's chocolate cake. "Looks good. You don't mind, do you?"

As Carol leaned over, Tom could smell her perfume. He looked at her, and for a split second, moved forward to kiss her. The decision was quickly taken out of his hands, and Carol moved back to her seat.

"I really enjoyed tonight, Tom, and it's been great seeing you!"

Tom was still thinking about the kiss, and he struggled to get a sentence out. "We just need Mike to get run over a bit more often!"

"Or you could just visit without the need for hospitalisation!"

Tom drank his coffee and gestured to the waiter for the bill.

Carol couldn't see the bill, but looked for a reaction in Tom's face. "Should I get my marigolds on?"

Tom looked up and smiled. "No, but when I say run, you run, okay?"

For a split second, and knowing Tom, she was unsure if he was being serious. She was relieved to see him place a pile of notes into an attractive, embossed leather wallet that the waiter had left.

It was expensive but worth every penny. "Should we walk back to yours?"

"Yes, good idea. We can walk some of this meal off!"

It was a cool evening, and Tom helped Carol put on her coat. The traffic was quiet, but as always in the city, there was a vibrant buzz. The streets were lined with drinkers heading out for a late night, as well as commuters heading for the last tube home, looking dishevelled in their suits.

Tom loved the city, but the appeal was not what it once was. He missed his life in the country. He liked the fact that he was important in his new world. The city had a habit of making you feel anonymous, lonely and unimportant, desensitized to a point. You would pass homeless people or drunks collapsed in a doorway and just simply move to one side to pass them. People seemed to care more in a small community, not just about the community itself, but also about those that they shared the community with. Many would find the transition difficult. Indeed, Tom could not have considered moving back to the country twelve months ago, but now life in the city was starting to feel alien to him.

He looked at Carol, and could see her cheeks and nose had a slight rose tint to them. He was unsure if this was the red wine or the cool air, but he offered his arm to her, and she gratefully linked his arm, pulling him closer. He could have easily thought of this as a romantic gesture, but he knew Carol was always cold; this was simply a way of stealing some of his body heat.

They didn't really speak on the walk back to the house, which was a little over a mile away. They were enjoying the walk, and happy to absorb the sights and smells of the city.

Tom was starting to feel a little nervous at the thought of getting back to the house. *Do I?* he thought to himself. He had really enjoyed the night, but he was unsure what to do. He cared for Carol, but he was now sure he wanted to be with her. He had no idea if she had any feelings for him, and he still didn't know if she was with anybody else. He hadn't felt like this before, and realised it was because he really liked Carol.

He used his key to open the front door and helped Carol take her coat off. She looked impressed. "I could get used to these manners, Tom."

"It's just a city persona. I'm a real slob when I get back to the country." He took his coat off and walked toward the kitchen. "One for the road?"

"Sure, why not? I wouldn't be saying this if we'd drunk that second bottle of wine."

He'd heard her, but wasn't really listening. There were several conversations running through his head, and he felt in turmoil. He'd taken a chance when he'd left the city, and he knew that if he wanted to be with her, the first step was to tell her.

He sat next to her on the sofa as his drink nearly slipped from his sweating hands. "I need to ask you something serious."

Carol looked a little concerned, and took a sip from her glass. "What is it?"

He paused for a moment, a voice in his head urging him to tell her how he felt. "Promise me you won't cry when you drink that wine!"

The voice inside his head screamed at him for bottling it.

Carol threw a cushion which bounced his arm. "I don't do that anymore!" she protested.

He had to move away, and looked through her music collection. "You have a really bad taste in music! Beautiful South, that'll do!"

He returned next to Carol on the sofa, and they both put their feet on the coffee table as she sang the words to "Perfect 10."

She had never been a good singer, but Tom looked at her and smiled. He was aware of what a good friend she was, and the realisation that he could ruin it filled him with dread. His head was pounding, as he knew the time to do something was tonight. If he didn't do anything, he wasn't sure he ever would. He thought to himself, *If she tells me to piss off, I can blame the wine!*

Carol stood up and moved toward the kitchen. Tom instinctively stood up as well, and was aware that she might think he was stalking her. He thought about pulling her close to him and tenderly kissing her, but he knew this wasn't a film, and things didn't work that way.

Instead, he stood behind Carol, who became aware that he wasn't moving and turned around to see what he was doing.

She looked at him for a moment, but he didn't move or speak. "You look a bit simple stood there!"

He was playing the scene in his head, and had momentarily forgotten that Carol was stood in front of him. He knew he had to do or say something, but he didn't know what.

He desperately tried to compose himself. "Look, I had actually asked Debbie Turner out tonight, but she was busy. I was hoping I would be giving Debbie a goodnight kiss tonight, but as she isn't here, I wondered if you would like to instead."

Carol looked at Tom for what felt like an eternity, and he could feel the beads of sweat dripping down his back. "How long have you had to come up with a line, and that's the best you can come up with?"

Tom smiled and wanted to run for the door, but even if he did he knew his legs would not have carried him.

Carol moved toward him. "As long as you don't tell Debbie, I don't mind!"

Tom leaned forward and gently guided her face toward his. He placed a hand on her face and kissed her, and it was as heavenly, better than he had imagined.

He took a step back to catch his breath. "This isn't weird, isn't it?"

Carol couldn't help but look at his crotch. "Kissing you isn't, but seeing you with one of them is!"

Tom looked embarrassed, but other than lie on the floor there was nothing he could do. "You're not drunk, are you?"

"Am I crying?" she asked.

"Good point!" he said, as he quickly grabbed her again.

She took him by the hand and led him toward her bedroom. "Wait there a moment."

She scoured the room, and quickly lit as many candles as she could find, while simultaneously hiding makeup bags, hairdryers and straighteners.

Tom stood outside the bedroom, preparing like a prizefighter. He was very aware that it had been a long time since he'd been with a girl, particularly one he was attracted to. He counted the drinks he'd had, desperately trying to calculate if the alcohol consumed would have the desired aesthetic effect.

Shit, what if I've drunk too much?

He tensed his stomach muscles and flexed his arms, desperate to garner extra muscle density to impress Carol, but he knew this was all but hopeless. He undid the top button on his borrowed shirt and stood dramatically in the doorway in an attempt to look seductive, but again, knew this was hopeless.

On the other side of the door, Carol desperately tried to find a matching set of underwear, but nothing. She had a clean set of pyjamas embossed with a Winnie the Pooh logo. *Cute?* she thought, before throwing them under her bed. She looked at her full laundry basket with anger. There was nothing else she could do other than jump into bed naked. She gave a quick squirt of her deodorant and nervously jumped into bed.

Tom was still stood in the doorway, desperately trying to retain his stance, although his stomach muscles were now starting to quiver.

"Come in," Carol said, desperately trying not to sound like a cross between a headmistress and the leading lady in a 1980's porn flick.

Tom took one final deep breath and opened the door. He felt awkward and unsure how he should perform basic human functions such as walking and where he should move his arms.

Should I get undressed? he thought, *or it that too presumptuous? She's in bed, of course it isn't presumptuous!*

He released the remaining buttons on his shirt and gently placed it on the end of the bed. He removed his belt while trying to slide his shoes off, struggling to retain his balance. The belt was soon removed, but the shoes would not budge. He was desperately trying to use one foot to force the other shoe off whilst trying to look seductive, with very limited success.

He reached down, but the shoes were tied in a double knot, and the forcing action had tightened them further. With no other option, he had to sit on the floor and desperately loosen his shoes. If he'd had a pair of scissors, he would have happily sliced the laces.

The shoes came undone, but the action of sitting down released the entire contents of his pockets over the laminate floor. Coins were now bouncing around the room as he removed his trousers and moved toward the bed.

Carol peered over the top of her duvet and waved her finger. "Socks!"

Tom couldn't remove his socks quick enough, and became very aware that his boxer shorts were not performing their duty and keeping him supported. He had passed the point of caring and rapidly removed his socks and jumped into bed.

Tom had a huge smile. "You're naked."

Carol looked under the cover. "You're not!"

Tom quickly removed his boxer shorts and put his arm around Carol, pulling her close.

"The way you took them shoes off, sexy," said Carol.

"My finest moves are yet to come!" he replied.

He didn't know why he'd said that, and rolled his eyes. He was desperate to impress Carol, and was becoming increasingly nervous.

He kissed her with every ounce of passion he could muster, his hands tentatively moving toward her breasts.

Shit, they're big! he thought. *Great!*

He gently caressed her before moving his hand onto her nipple. Carol instantly reacted and pushed herself closer toward him. He kissed the side of her neck and moved his hands down her back, softly brushing the top of her thigh.

"Have you got a condom?" she asked.

Tom had that moment of panic you only get when you realise you've lost your phone or your wallet. He knew he didn't have one, but he mentally visualised every possible place there could be one, and knew it was hopeless.

"No. Do you? Please say you do!"

"No! Sorry!" He gave a gentle sigh, calm on the exterior, but inside he was screaming at himself. Although in his defence he didn't imagine he'd end up in bed with Carol, he had imagined it, several times; he just didn't think it could actually happen.

Carol laughed to break the tension. "Maybe next time?"

"Next time I'll have a condom, I promise!" said Tom.

"Can you bring one more thing next time?" she asked. "Bring slip-on shoes!"

Chapter Five

Una Jacob looked intently at her newspaper, a picture of Clint staring back at her. Clint had capitalised on his brief resurgence by finally releasing his autobiography, and his song used in the TV advert had appealed to a new generation, resulting in the song being re-released.

"Suzie, get me that piece of shit Clint Lee on the phone!"

She paced her office dressed in an immaculate black designer suit as she read the rest of the article. Her hair was tied back in a bun, but she looked elegant rather than frumpy.

"Clint on line one, Una."

"Clint Lee, you've lost weight. That's good! I'm looking at you in the paper today, and I like what I see!"

"Oh, fuck off, Una, I haven't heard from you for weeks. You're only phoning because I'm back in the charts!"

"Of course I am. Why else would I be phoning a degenerate deadbeat like you?"

Clint was about to hang up the phone, but he liked the fact that Una had phoned him. He'd lost count of the number of times she'd refused to take his calls, so was intrigued as to why she was now phoning him.

"Look, you remember last time I said I didn't like you? Well, I still don't! The truth is, I'm in the business of making money, making a deadbeat like you *not* a deadbeat. Don't for one minute think that your song in the charts is going to place you back on easy street, because honey, it isn't. Are you off the booze?"

Clint listened to Una intently and clenched his fist. "Yes, I'm off the booze, and I've lost a couple of stone."

"I'm looking at you in the paper. You look good! How are the book sales?"

Clint paused for a moment. "Flying, Una, it's going really well."

"Don't bullshit me, Clint. You forget that I can see how many books you've sold. You should have spoken to me before you released the book. Give me twenty percent and I'll get you in the top ten. Also, I don't want to see you in the paper stood next to other deadbeat comeback kings. It isn't good for your image. If you don't want to be a deadbeat, don't hang about with deadbeats!"

Clint had a confused tone in his voice. "Do you actually still work for me?"

"No, honey, you work for me, and the sooner you realise that, the sooner we make money. Remember, I don't like you because you don't make me money. If you make me money I will like you, and there are a lot of wealthy people out there who like me, Clint. There are also a lot of losers out there that don't like me. Do you want me to like you, Clint?"

The conversation was like a whirlwind, and Clint was unsure who worked for who. "I think so, Una?"

"Good, and don't think any more. That's my job! I take twenty percent of anything you make, and I mean anything, Clint. Don't fuck me over, Clint, I know everything. Lay off the booze and the pizzas, and don't hang around with deadbeats!"

Clint felt like he was being spoken to like a naughty child. "Okay, Una. Do you look after any bands? Eighties' bands, that sort of thing?"

"Clint, if I can make money out of them, I would get Elvis to sing with the Rat Pack."

The phone went dead, and Clint stood looking puzzled, trying to take stock of what had just happened. Una had that ability to control and manipulate people, and at this moment, Clint felt well and truly manipulated.

Tom opened one eye. He knew he was lying next to Carol, but wondered if it was some cruel trick his mind was playing on him. Carol lay with her back to him, her hair still immaculate from the night before. He took a moment to appreciate the moment, and could scarcely believe that he was lying next to Carol.

He moved toward her and whispered in her ear. "Morning, Carol."

Carol groaned. "Oh no, I thought it was a bad dream!" Tom recoiled like he'd been smashed in the face, but was relieved as Carol rolled over with a huge smile. "Morning Tom, I hope you're taking me somewhere equally as posh for breakfast?"

"I've got you in bed now," he said, jumping out of bed. "It's pot noodles and corn flakes from here on in!"

He climbed into the shower and thought about the events of the previous night and how much he enjoyed being with Carol. The only negative was the two-hour drive between them.

Once they were ready, Carol took him to a café next to the hospital, where virtually all of the customers were uniformed hospital staff.

He casually looked around the café. "So this is where all the nurses hang out? I must remember that!"

"Only the fat ones," Carol whispered. "Do you want to talk about last night? Any regrets?"

Tom shook his head. "My only regret is that I didn't have a condom."

She smiled as the man on the adjacent table looked over. "Are we okay, though?"

"I'm more than okay, Carol! I'm more okay now than I have been for a long time. Carol, I like you, I mean, *really* like you!"

Carol smiled and poured him a cup of tea.

"So was it a onetime thing?" he asked.

Carol looked offended. "Do I look like a onetime kind of girl?"

"Well, yes! That's what attracted me to you!"

She pretended to look offended. "I didn't expect anything to happen, if I'm being honest. If I woke up this morning and it felt weird, then I'd probably have said it was a onetime thing. But, it didn't feel weird. It felt nice and comfortable. So if you want to take me out on a date again, and I didn't have a better offer, I'd probably say yes. It would have to be to an equally extravagant restaurant, though!"

"Last night was just to lure you in. McDonald's drive-thru next time!"

Carol finished her tea and paid for breakfast.

"Thank you for the gourmet breakfast," said Tom.

"Don't thank me," she said. "I picked all your change up off the floor, so I should be thanking you!"

Tom opened the door for her, and they walked toward the hospital. He extended his hand, and to his surprise, Carol willingly accepted. "Maybe later we can put our hands in each other's back pocket?"

She walked past a number of her work colleagues and smiled. Tom was pleased because she continued to hold his hand, so wasn't embarrassed to be seen with him. As they approached the ward where Mike was admitted, they saw two uniformed policemen leaving his room.

Carol panicked, and was relieved to see Mike sat up in his bed. She entered his room with a warm smile. "Morning, Mike, you look so much better today!"

Mike pushed himself up on his bed. "Morning, guys, it's great to see you both. Nice shirt, Tom."

"Cheers, mate. Thanks for lending it to me! I wore your cheeky blue number last night as well. The ladies loved it." Tom briefly looked at Carol, then back at Mike. "What did the police say?"

Mike spoke quietly. "They caught the person who crashed into me."

Carol moved closer to the bed. "That's great news!" Mike didn't reply, and put his head back on his pillow, so she adjusted her tone. "Oh. *Not* great?"

Mike shook his head. "No, not great at all."

Tom looked confused. "If they've caught them, how is that not good?"

"There was no CCTV in the area, so the police checked the buses that have CCTV, and a bus coming toward me caught the whole thing on camera: the van swerved toward me!"

"Shit," said Tom. "Deliberate?"

Mike nodded slowly. "Very deliberate!"

Carol sat down on the chair next to his bed and looked at the floor. "Why the hell would anyone try and run you over? I don't understand it."

"The police gave me the name of the guy who was driving," said Mike, "but it meant nothing to me. Eventually they showed me a photograph they'd taken when the guy was brought into custody."

Mike took a long pause, to the frustration of Tom. "And...?"

Mike composed himself. "It took me a while, but I eventually recognised him. Do you remember that girl I brought home? The girl I worked with?"

Carol looked blankly and shrugged her shoulders.

"She was noisy. You said you heard her making all sorts of noises?"

Carol nodded her head. "I do now, but that was ages ago, and what has she got to do with this? Were you that bad in bed she wanted to run you over?"

Mike shook his head. "No, she was happy, but her husband wasn't when he found out. I'd heard he was a nutter, but I assumed he wouldn't find out."

"Fuck," said Tom. "What did the police say?"

"I didn't tell them. I said I didn't recognise him."

Carol stood up and looked at Mike. "You said you didn't know him? Why the hell would you say that if he tried to kill you!"

"This guy is nuts! He told the police the sun blinded him and it was all an accident, and they've already said it would be difficult to prove it wasn't an accident. If I grass him up and he still gets a slap on the wrist, who is he coming looking for?"

"So what now, though?" asked Tom. "What if he comes after you again?"

"I'm kind of hoping he's got it out of his system, and to be fair to him, I did shag his wife!"

"Yes, but almost killing you! Jesus, she was a pig anyway. You were doing him a favour!"

"I agree, but you can tell him that!"

Carol shook her head in disbelief. "This is crazy. You cannot just let this nutter get away with attempted murder!"

Mike looked dejected. "There isn't much I can do!"

"I kind of agree," said Tom. "If the police can't prove it was anything other than an accident, the guy walks. What you need him to know is that you could have grassed him up, but you didn't!"

Carol sat back down. "This is a mess! You cannot look over your shoulder for the rest of your life. This idiot needs to be locked up. What if he kills you next time?"

Tom moved toward Carol and put a reassuring hand on her shoulder. "What about work, Mike? You can't go back working with that girl."

Mike shook his head. "Not a chance am I going back there! I will drag out the recovery from this. Work should pay me for a few months, and I'll just hand my notice in. Looking back, I'm sure that nutter's been following me. You know you get that feeling you're being followed, but you just brush it off?"

Carol placed her hand on Mike's, and smiled. "You look a lot better today. Did they give you an indication of how long you would be in for?"

"Thanks! It's not as bad as it looks, and they're pleased with my progress. Probably a couple of more days."

"I'll be heading back later today, mate," said Tom. "But if you fancy getting away from it all, we've always got space for you. Only twelve quid a night and I'll throw a sleeping bag in!"

Mike laughed, but grimaced as he did so. "I might take you up on that, but we'll call it quits on the shirt hire."

"Hang on a minute," said Carol. "So some nutter is trying to kill you, and presumably knows where you live, in my house, and you're thinking of doing one out to the country, leaving me alone?"

Tom looked at Mike. "Shit, Carol's got a point there! If he knows where you live, what's to stop him coming 'round? This guy needs to be told to back off, otherwise…"

"Otherwise what, Tom? Therein lies the problem. What can I do? I am not exactly going to intimidate this guy!"

"You were brave enough to tackle his wife, though!" said Tom with a wry smile. "Look, what about I go and speak with him? When I say go and speak with him, I mean phone, possibly text!"

"No offence, Tom, but you are about as intimidating as me. Carol would probably be more forceful."

Carol looked at Tom and Mike. "All you need is this guy to know it's over, finished! And I have to agree, you two are not what I would call intimidating."

Tom thought for a moment, and then a small epiphany came to him. "Larry!"

Mike looked at him blankly. "Who's Larry?"

"Larry, my old boss who owns the bookies. He's an absolute nutter!"

Carol stood up, looking bemused. "What good is getting one nutter to speak with another nutter?"

"No, Carol, when I say nutter, I mean a proper nutter. Not a nutter who can swing a punch, but a full-on-torture kind of nutter, like you see in the films. I can ask him to politely tell your friend that all of this is now over, no police, just finished. Trust me, if this guy tells you it's over, it's over!"

Carol shook her head and walked toward the door. "I'm not listening to this. I'm going to get some coffees."

"Larry is the kind of guy that does things for money, though. So it'll cost," said Tom.

"How much?" asked Mike.

"No idea. I can give him a phone and put you in touch with him?"

Mike was nervous. "Shit, this is like something from *The Sopranos.* I'm boring, Mike, what am I doing getting involved with gangsters?"

"You're not. Well, not yet— He might say no!"

Mike sat back on his bed and closed his eyes. He knew Tom was right, and if he didn't do something, then he'd always be looking over his shoulder. Even worse, what if the husband did come around when Carol was in?

Mike thought for a while. "Can you give him a call and see if he'll do it?"

"Sure, I'll give him a call before I leave today."

Carol walked back into the room and handed a coffee to Mike and Tom. "I'm not asking!"

Mike's face was swollen and bruised, and despite his best efforts to hide it, a tear rolled down his cheek. "I'm sorry, guys. I didn't think this would happen, and I didn't want to get you involved."

Carol moved toward him and held his hand. "We know," she said reassuringly. "But promise me one thing? If you go out drinking again, please keep your nob in your pants?"

Mike laughed, but again the movement caused him to grimace with pain.

"I'm working tonight, so I'll drop in later on, see how you're doing?"

"Thanks, Carol, that'd be great. Can you bring me in a few things from the house: undies, that sort of thing? A shirt maybe, if I've got any left!"

Tom walked over to Mike and gently pressed his shoulder. "Look after yourself, buddy. I'll call you later?"

"Yeah, see you, guys, and thanks for everything!"

Tom walked out of the ward before putting his arm around Carol. He'd wanted to say something to Mike, but was conscious that he had more pressing matters on his mind. He thought about Larry, and had that moment of doubt that you feel when you make an offer in good faith, but once you've had time to digest it, wish you hadn't.

Tom went back to the house with Carol, and packed the few things he'd brought with him back into the car. He was looking forward to going, but knew that he'd miss Carol. He always missed Carol, but this time it was different.

He stood next to his car and pulled her close to him. "I'm going to miss you, Carol, really miss you!"

She stood on her toes and kissed him. "Can you come back on Saturday, spend the weekend here? Hopefully Mike will be out of the hospital and we can catch up?"

Tom looked at her, and for a moment didn't want to go. "Sure! I'll give you a call tonight. I know I muck around and don't take things seriously, but I'm turning things around, Carol. I promise you, I will not mess you around. I like you and I want to be with you!"

Carol smiled. "I know. Call me later!"

He drove away as she waved from the house and blew a solitary kiss.

The miles passed in a blur as Tom thought about everything that had happened. He felt relief that Mike was going to be fine, and couldn't stop thinking about Carol and how things would work out.

What about this distance? he thought. If things worked out, he considered if he should move back to the city. The problem was, he liked his new life and was reluctant to move back, but he also really wanted to make it work with Carol.

He pulled into the campsite and was pleased to see that it was relatively busy. There was no sign of Ricky in the office, so he took the short walk to the top end of the field where the new cabins were being built. Although he'd only been away for a short while, Ricky had made real progress on the cabins.

Ricky leaned from the window and gestured toward his work on the cabin, and Tom raised his hand in appreciation. "How's Mike?" shouted Ricky.

"Good! I'll take you for a pint after, and tell you all about it. I'll be in the office, I need to make a call."

Tom walked slowly toward the office, running through different scenarios in his mind. *Do I do this?* he thought. His mind turned back to Mike lying in that hospital bed, and Carol being alone in the house. He knew that this situation had to end, and end now.

Do I really want to get involved with Larry?

"Oh my god! Clint Lee! It is, it's Clint Lee!" the voice screamed.

Clint spun around and raised his hands for defence rather than attack. *Whose voice?* he quickly thought, but he didn't recognise it.

"Can we get a selfie, Clint?"

Clint was taken off balance, but he realised his potential assailants were two teenage girls smiling eagerly at him. The last time Clint was accosted for a picture in the street, mobile phones were in their infancy.

"Sure!" he said with a beaming smile. "Go for it."

Clint looked at himself in his young admirer's phone, pleased that he'd taken the time to shave that morning.

"My mum loves you. Wait till she sees this!"

Clint smiled but felt momentarily dejected. "Thanks, girls, take care!" he said warmly. "Tell your mum I said a big hello!"

He soon reasoned that it doesn't matter who likes you as long as someone does. It had not been that long since Clint was lying face down on the floor of his flat and now people were coming up to him in the street again.

Clint had always got a buzz from people coming up to him. Some celebrities detest it, but when it goes, they all miss it. Meeting Carol had been a real event for him. Yes, he knew nothing would ever happen, but it had given him a renewed motivation to get his life back on track. The two girls recognising him had given him a spring in his step.

The money was starting to come in for Clint, and Una, true to her word, was starting to make things happen. He was starting to appear in the papers, not with deadbeats, but established household names.

"Don't be seen with deadbeats!" Una would constantly drill into him.

He still didn't like Una, and he was frustrated about the twenty percent commission, but Clint wasn't stupid: eighty percent of something is better than one hundred percent of nothing. The press was more positive toward him; feel-good stories were appearing, not rehashed clichés of the former pop star who had it all.

Una was a specialist at drip-feeding just the right stories to the press, which Clint realised was where Una really earned her commission. He was acutely aware that Una had the ability to make it all disappear with the click of an email or a call to the right ears.

With the renewed interest in him, the book sales had started to fly, and as Una had promised, the book was now firmly rooted in the top ten.

"Success is momentum! We need to keep building on it!" Una would often say to him, and she was right.

Clint was now starting to get nervous, and he adjusted his suit jacket and straightened his tie repeatedly. He took a deep breath to compose himself, pausing briefly. He then opened the door with purpose and vigour.

"Studio three, please?"

The security guard behind the desk looked up and pointed in the direction of the large studio three sign above his head, and smiled.

Clint made his way through an array of doors to Studio Three, where he was met by an excitable young researcher named Emma.

"Clint, welcome!" beamed Emma. She was pretty and dressed well, but had a smile that was obviously false. She ushered Clint into a small waiting room. "No surprises, Clint, I promise. The questions we sent to your house are the questions you'll be getting asked. Between me and you, the girls can be a bit saucy. You just need to go with it, give them a taste of their own medicine!"

Clint had been on TV numerous times, but he was nervous. He was desperately trying to get back into the public arena, and he was unsure if Una had picked the wrong show for him to make his rejuvenated debut.

Coffee Break was a chat show hosted by three women and an overly camp former politician. The panel could be vicious, and would often lead to car-crash TV, but the public watched it.

"Sorry I'm late!" boomed Una as she stormed into the room. "Emma, if you set him up, I promise you I will ruin your career!"

Clint looked a little shocked, although a little impressed at the same time. Una was formidable despite her demure stature. She looked elegant in a matching suit jacket and skirt, but Clint wondered if the soulless black colour was a deliberate choice to accentuate her cold persona.

Emma wasn't fazed by the grand entrance, and stood her ground well. "Una, an enormous pleasure as always! I was just explaining to Clint that the panel won't ask any questions that you haven't been advised of."

Una had now turned her attention to Clint, and her back to Emma. "Don't improvise, don't think you're funny, and don't try to crack jokes. You are *not* funny! Stick to the script and you'll be fine. I've seen people die on this show. It can kill you but it can make you. If this goes well, your book will be at number one, the phone will be ringing, and people will want to be seen with you. Fuck it up and you're history!"

Clint, who was already feeling nervous, now felt sick. Emma gave him a pity smile, although he was unsure if this was for the show or his association with Una.

"Makeup, and then we should be on in about twenty minutes. Always a pleasure, Una!" Emma said sarcastically as she left the room.

Clint now felt like he was going in for an operation, waiting for the nurse to take him to get anaesthetic. The show was live with a studio audience, and as Una had pointed out, it could make or break him. Una didn't like small talk, and so made no effort to do so. She scanned her blackberry and made no attempt to put Clint at ease, although he knew there was very little anyone could do to calm his nerves.

He had his makeup applied, and was led out to the stage floor where he could see an audience of about 100 people. The panel members were lit up in the centre of the stage, surrounded by an array of cameras and people milling around out of shot of the camera.

Clint felt a solitary bead of sweat run down his forehead. He had rehearsed what he was going to say, and had been confident. Now he had little faith in his legs to navigate the short walk to the stage. He wanted to run. It was like a surreal dream.

"We are very pleased to have the former West End musical star and musician, Clint Lee!"

The audience began to cheer, but Clint didn't move. He felt like he was instructing his legs to move, but they didn't. Emma rushed over and literally pushed him forward like a lamb to the slaughter, and forced a smile as he wiped the bead of sweat from his forehead. He waved to the audience, and carefully made his way to his seat next to the camp ex-politician called Peter.

True to their word, the panel members were positive, and spent time talking about his book and plans for the future. The only awkward moment came when Peter brought up his drinking, albeit the subject was covered in his book.

Clint handled it well. "I feel like I know you guys with the amount of time I spent watching your show in the afternoons, nursing a bottle of whiskey. In fact, Peter, you actually look better after half a bottle of whiskey!"

He became suddenly aware of Una`s advice not to try and be funny. He froze for a moment, and to his massive relief the audience began to applaud. Peter smiled. "That's what the Prime Minister used to say to me as well!"

Una watched the interview in a separate room, and while she treated Clint with contempt, she didn't want him to fail. Not just because of the money, but because she knew he probably wouldn't cope well with further rejection.

The interview was short, and the audience showed him warm appreciation. He took a huge gasp of air and walked into the room where Una was waiting.

"Don't be funny, I said, and what do you do?" barked Una, which inspired in Clint a look of real disappointment. Una sensed the dejection, and for a moment showed him something close to compassion. "You looked good, Clint. You came across well."

Her compassion was as short-lived as her patience. "What is this charity work you were talking about? What concert? Charity work does not pay you a bean, you do it when you have enough cash to give your time away!"

Clint looked at her in desperation. "You told me to do something, and I thought this would help?"

"Thinking again, honey! I told you to let me do the thinking. Now you'll have to do a load of charity work, for which you don't get paid!"

Clint had backed himself into a corner, once again not taking Una`s advice and moving away from the scripted answers he had rehearsed countless times in his head. During the interview he had suggested that he wanted to get involved in raising money for charity, hoping that this could only improve his profile. He was asked what projects he was getting involved in, and the only project he could think of was the music festival that Tom has discussed with him.

A charity music concert! Why the fuck did I say that? thought Clint. *Of all the things I could have said, shit!*

Una shook her head. "Anyway, kid, that's your problem. Aside from that, you did well. I've got a meeting with someone to discuss some potential stage work for you!"

Clint's face lit up. "No way! That would be fantastic, Una! Doing what?"

"Too early to say but I'll keep you posted. I need to go. I would give you a lift but I'm not going to. Speak soon!"

She left as quickly as she had arrived.

Emma walked back into the room. "Oh, did I miss her? What a shame! See, I told you they wouldn't stitch you up. We're all about entertaining our audience, not humiliating our guests."

"It went well. I quite enjoyed it once I got into it. Sorry about Una. She can be a bit—"

"Of an arrogant bitch?"

Clint laughed. "Yes, that's probably quite a polite way of putting it!"

"We all know Una, don't worry about it. She's like that all the time. She's just looking out for you."

"She has a funny way of showing she cares, I'd hate to see what she's like when she *doesn't* care! Anyway, thanks!"

"No problem, you came across well. I heard you were all washed up, on the piss all the time. But you look well, better than I thought you would. Good luck with the book and the concert. I would love to go to that, let me know when it is. Here, take a business card."

Clint left the studio elated. It had been a good day for him. He thought about the stage opportunity Una had mentioned and how he would love to get back to working in the theatre.

His thoughts returned to the charity concert he'd just committed to on live TV, and he wondered if it would be forgotten about. But that was a risk he couldn't take. Promising to do something for charity and not delivering could be terminal for his career.

Shit! he thought. *Why did I say that?*

He paused for a moment to compose his thoughts. As he did this, he pulled out his phone and scrolled through his contact list. He was pleased to see that he'd saved the number.

I need to phone Tom later! he thought.

Ricky headed toward the office to find Tom. He had been working all day, and was now looking forward to the pint that Tom had promised him.

"Pint?" he asked, but Tom was looking preoccupied and a little pale.

"Yes, but can I meet you down there? Give me ten minutes. I need to give Mike a quick call." Ricky gave an understanding nod before heading back out of the office. Tom brought his phone to his ear. "Pick up, Mike!" he said aloud, pacing around the office. Finally, he heard Mike's voice on the other end. "Mike, it's me. Larry is going to sort it. He's going to have a word. You just need to give him some details about this guy. Will you call him?"

Mike was relieved, although, like Tom, he was nervous about getting involved with someone like Larry. "How much is it going to cost?"

Tom listened to Mike, but was frustrated. "No, Mike, it won't cost you anything, but that Clint Lee has dropped me right in the shit."

Mike was confused and beginning to sense the frustration in Tom's voice. "I don't understand. What does Clint Lee have to do with this?"

"Larry has just seen him on TV, banging on about some concert he's putting on. I told Larry the other day that I was trying to put something together with Clint Lee, and Larry was keen to throw some cash at it. Now he really wants to get involved, but this time he doesn't want to throw any cash at it. He just wants twenty percent of what this concert makes, and in return he sorts out your little problem!"

"Shit," said Mike.

Tom was in a panic. "Shit is right! A gangster, a washed-up alcoholic one-hit wonder, no money and no acts! What could possibly go wrong?"

Chapter Six

Clint pulled up a chair next to the fire, and took a mouthful from his glass of coke, looking longingly at other customers enjoying a cold lager. He thought of Emma, the pretty research assistant, and checked his wallet to make sure that he'd not misplaced her business card. At the height of his career, Clint was well used to seductive gazes being thrown at him, but he was unsure if Emma was simply being friendly and professional. His radar for such matters had long since eroded, damaged by years of pity and disdain.

As his popularity had increased, his self-confidence had also grown, which in turn had prompted a change in the public, or at least in how they reacted to him.

Pope stood behind the bar, periodically looking at Clint, struggling to place the face. He was sure he recognised him, but just couldn't figure out from where.

The lounge door opened and Clint instinctively turned around. "Tom, good to see you!"

"Two pints, please, Pope. Ricky'll be here in a minute."

Tom looked at Clint, and was impressed at how well he looked. He'd lost more weight, and was dressed sharp. Tom felt a little underdressed in combat shorts and a hooded top. "We need to put a concert on, then!" he said, getting straight to the point.

Clint smiled. "You were going to do it anyway, and I've just given you a push in the right direction!"

Tom took a deep breath to compose himself. "Okay, the situation is this. You, for reasons beyond my comprehension, have promised on live TV that you are doing a charity concert, correct?" Clint nodded in agreement. "Okay," continued Tom. "Saying that you're going to do a concert has set in place a further chain of events. I now have a business partner who is also very keen that I should do this concert. The difficulty is that he wants twenty percent of whatever the concert makes, and is going to put no money forward to fund the concert. Your problem is that you've committed to do this on live TV, and if you do not, presumably you'll end up back on skid row?"

Clint nodded. "Yes, pretty much. I wanted to do something nice."

Tom looked in amazement before laughing. "Did-you-fuck, Clint, you don't give two hoots about charity. You just want to get back in the newspapers!"

Clint looked hurt, and shook his head before pausing for a moment. "Yeah, you're right, Tom, I fucked up. I should have gone for something smaller scale, charity beach clean, one of those simpletons that pack your bag in the supermarket, that sort of thing. Look, Tom, if I cock this up, the press will have a field day. They would love to see me drowning in my own piss again."

"You said this was going to be a charity concert, and I can promise you it isn't. If I'm putting my neck on the line, I am not doing it for charity. You can give *your* share to charity, but you need to make that clear from the outset. Fair enough?" Clint nodded. "We need cash to do this," continued Tom. "How much can you throw in?"

Clint thought for a moment. "Five grand."

"Five grand," choked Tom. "Your career is over if this doesn't work out. Five grand! Try again, sunshine, or you can find some other idiot with the land and a campsite!"

Clint tapped a few numbers. "Twenty grand! But that is it. And I need that back!"

"Any money we put in we get back. Any money left over after expenses is the profit, which we will then allocate out," explained Tom. "Twenty percent goes to my business partner, and me and you will take thirty percent each. You can do what you want with your share: give it to charity, whatever!"

"Who is your business partner?" asked Clint. "And why are they getting twenty percent if they're not putting any cash in?"

Tom looked at Clint with a serious expression. "You don't need to know about him! I can put about fifteen grand in, and we have a further twenty percent we can sell. I provide the land and the accommodation. We need your expertise to get the stage and the acts sorted. I know just the people who can help me with the books and the advertising."

"But twenty percent for doing nothing?" protested Clint.

"That's the deal, my friend, take it or leave it. I'll be honest. I could do without this hassle!"

Clint chewed on his lip for a moment in rumination. Finally, he clapped his hands together in a moment of decisiveness. "Okay, let's do it."

"Do what?" asked Ricky, who had entered the pub and was approaching their table. He sat down and took a sip from his pint.

"The concert," explained Tom. "We're going into the music business!"

Clint continued to push buttons on his phone. "This budget is going to be a bit tight. Even if we do well with advance ticket sales, we're going to struggle to get any big names for this sort of cash!"

Tom was frustrated. "We spoke about this before, Clint, and we know we cannot get the big boys. What about the one-hit wonders? Think about it. Everyone loves those one-hit wonders. They must do, otherwise they would never've had a hit. The only reason people don't pay to see them is because they only have one hit. But if we have *several* one-hit wonders, the line-up should be strong enough to get people through the door."

"That could work," said Clint. "It would keep the costs down, and chances are they won't be booked in advance."

Tom tapped his fingers on the table. "We need a name, something catchy to get the punters in!"

Ricky looked thoughtful, and Clint and Tom waited in anticipation. "Dead-Beatz," said Ricky. "You know, like deadbeats."

Tom looked at Ricky and rolled his eyes. "Yeah, we get it, but I'm not sure Clint will be too pleased with that name, bearing in mind he'll be singing as well."

Ricky chuckled. "What about Dud-Stock? Anyway, stop saying 'concert.' It sounds shit. It's a *festival!*"

"Clint Lee Featuring the One-Hit Wonders!" suggested Clint.

Ricky nodded. "That could work, and it says exactly what it is."

"What about, *Clint Lee Presents the One-Hit Wonders*?" asked Tom.

Clint and Ricky looked at each other and nodded approvingly.

"Great!" said Tom. "And I think I have just thought of our final investor." He gave a broad smile and raised his glass toward Pope, who was covertly listening in on the conversation.

"Pope, come on over here. Let me introduce you to Clint. We've got a little proposition for you," said Tom, gesturing Pope to join them. "And bring another round over, we're celebrating!"

Pope didn't require much persuasion, and was happy to get involved. He'd seen how Tom operated, and was confident that it would be a success. Tom was pleased to have Pope on board. And not just for the cash he was injecting. He knew that Pope's influence in the village would be a real asset in getting the required support from the town council to put the event on.

The new consortium celebrated their collaboration over several more drinks, before moving to the campsite, so Pope and Clint could visualise the layout.

Clint walked around the site with excitement. "This place could take thousands!"

"It can take thousands," said Tom, "but getting them in the door in the first place is the tricky bit. Don't forget, this could be an annual event. As long as we all make a few quid, we can build on it. Clint, make sure the charity angle is only for this year!"

"No danger. That will be made abundantly clear. The way I figure it, if I can throw the charity five-to-ten K, that should get me some good press, and what I give, I'll get back from book sales."

"What about parking?" asked Ricky. "If we get hundreds of people turning up, where are they going to park?"

"We can sort out the finer details later," said Tom. "What we need to do first is get the acts booked, then we can start advertising and selling tickets. We were joking about deadbeats, Clint, but are there any *good* acts out there?"

"Sure there is," replied Clint. "The good ones will want to do this. It'll showcase them, give them another bite of the apple. I just need to make sure we steer clear of the ones with too much baggage — the pisspots and the ones that are going to cause us trouble. I can have a word with my agent. She's a bitch, but she knows everyone, and she'll let me know who's available, for how much, and whether they're going to cause us any trouble."

"We need to decide as a group, though, you know, regarding who we're going to book," said Pope.

Clint nodded. "No problem." He was pleased it would be a joint decision, as the choice of the acts would ultimately determine if the festival sold tickets. His confidence was improving, but he was pleased he'd have the input of others, and share the blame if it didn't work out. He knew that most of the money he'd earn would be given away, but he was looking at the bigger picture. He didn't want to give money away, but the way he figured it, he was investing in his future, a future that didn't exist a short while before.

105

"Come on. Let's head back down to the pub!" suggested Tom. "Clint, you can kip in one of the cabins, save you rushing back?"

As they headed back toward the pub, Tom began to think of Carol. He'd seen her the weekend before, and they'd spoken most nights, but he wanted her to be a part of this, part of his life.

"So, Clint, you looking forward to singing again?" asked Ricky.

"Definitely not!" said Clint with a chuckle. "The last time I was on stage, someone threw a live chicken at me."

"Impressive!" said Ricky.

"It was. I often wonder how long they were holding it for, and how they got it in. I can imagine them telling their mates how they threw a chicken at Clint Lee. It was at a low point, but I do chuckle about it now."

"Stick that jukebox on, will you, Pope?" asked Tom. "Let's get a few of those one-hit wonders on the go. Do a bit of market research!"

As the pub filled, the atmosphere grew, and Tom continued to observe the punters, noting which songs provoked a reaction, and which didn't. There was a good cross-section of age groups in the pub, and he knew that to make the festival work, they would need to appeal to all of them.

"Why don't we get together before I go back to the city?" asked Clint. "We can run through the names we want, and I can take that away with me. Plus it'll save me from coming back during the week?"

"Great!" said Tom. "Come on. I'll show you where you're sleeping."

Pope was virtually asleep in his seat, as Ricky and Tom escorted Clint back to the hut.

"Give me a call if you need anything," said Tom, who paused for a moment. "I'm looking forward to this, Clint, really looking forward to it!"

Clint sat in the dark, and laughed as he recalled the incident with the chicken. He now found it amusing, and used it as a benchmark of his lowest point. He was drinking heavily, and taking any work, regardless of the standard. If he ever felt down, he would think back to that time to make him realise what low really meant, and how his life was now heading in the right direction.

He had forgotten what it was like to have people respect and value his opinion. He enjoyed spending time with Ricky and Tom, and was determined to make things work, and not just for the money. His self-respect was returning, and of all his deserted friends, this was the one he missed the most.

Tom and Ricky took the short walk toward their cabins. Ricky had virtually completed the left-hand cabin, meaning that Tom could now move out of the small camping hut that had felt like his home for months.

"I'm proud of you for doing this," said Tom.

Ricky put his arm around his brother. "And you're pissed!"

"Yeah, a little pissed," said Tom, smiling. "But I mean it, about what you've done here." Ricky remained silent and humble, rarely the type to gloat about his hard work. "Ricky," continued Tom, "what do you think of Clint?"

Ricky thought for a moment. "Yeah, he seems okay."

"Do you think we can trust him?"

"I do. Why?"

"We can make big money if this goes well, but if it goes tits up, we can lose a lot of cash. We need to put a lot of trust in a person we don't really know." Tom felt a weight of responsibility on his shoulders, partly towards Ricky, but he had also got Pope involved. Pope was not stupid, though, and was an experienced businessman. Tom knew the man wouldn't get involved if he had any doubts. The fact that Pope had embraced the idea so willingly had given Tom a real confidence boost. Tom looked at Ricky and raised his glass. "Me and you, in the music business!"

"To the one-hit wonders!"

Clint woke up early, and the unusual surroundings inspired in him a moment of panic. He'd been no stranger to waking up in unfamiliar places, wondering where the previous day had gone.

He composed his thoughts, and was grateful for the lack of a hangover. Last night, he'd found being around drinkers difficult, and wanted to make a concerted effort to stay away from any temptations. If his life was in balance, he was confident that he could drink again socially, without it being a problem, but for now, he enjoyed not having alcohol in his life.

There was little sign of life on the campsite, so Clint took the opportunity to take a walk through the village. The feel of this rural community was something he'd never experienced. It was stunning. He stopped briefly to buy a coffee from the shop and continued his walk toward the reservoir.

Clint felt like he had been transported to the nineteenth century, and was captivated by the thatched cottages draped in ivy, surrounded by ornate picket fences. Instantly he could see the appeal of living in the country, and could now understand why people in the city sell up to start a new life. Clint enjoyed the social life of the city, but without drinking there was nothing for him aside from work.

He felt deafened by the silence, which was usually drowned out by throngs of people pushing past, coupled with the clogged arteries of traffic. His thoughts of the city were quickly removed as he rounded a corner and caught sight of the reservoir. The sight before him took his breath away, as he was greeted with a vast expanse of tranquil water surrounded by sweeping hills.

He pushed open a gate and walked a few steps to take him to the entrance of the reservoir. Walking down another set of stairs, he came down toward the edge of the water and passed a marker post indicating that the winter rain had not yet replenished the summer use.

It would take years to truly appreciate the beauty of the landscape before him, but Clint desperately absorbed what he could. He had a strange feeling, something he'd not felt for years. He felt at peace, like he was on the cusp of something, like he was emerging from a long sleep.

He continued to walk further around the reservoir, and this feeling of tranquillity brought him focus. The years behind him were just that: behind him. It was a cliché, but he felt alive, like he had a new awakening, full of renewed vigour. For the first time in his life it was a struggle to find a negative. His thoughts were positive and full of ambition, and he loved it!

Clint could have stayed there all day, but his thoughts turned back toward the music festival. They had arranged to meet at nine a.m., giving them time to discuss acts before he needed to head back to the city. However, being the only sober person, he was not confident of their attendance.

His concern was soon allayed when he saw Pope outside the pub, pacing like a wildcat. Once he saw Clint, the landlord virtually ran toward him. "I couldn't sleep last night!"

Clint looked a little surprised, and smiled. "You were asleep when I left!"

"Well, I woke up. I've been on the internet all night looking at music videos." Pope had the excitement and enthusiasm of a small child.

"Let's have a look, then!" said Clint, matching the enthusiasm.

Tom was standing next to the bar, nursing a cup of coffee, and Ricky sat reading a newspaper. "I've printed off a list of artists classified as one-hit wonders. There's a copy for each of you. I've highlighted the ones I think are good, and put a line through the ones that are shit, I mean proper shit!"

Tom was also pleasantly surprised by the enthusiasm, and this also made him feel a little easier about asking Pope to get involved. It was obvious that he knew what he was doing, and was going into this with his eyes wide open.

The four business partners pulled two tables together, and sat like the *X-Factor* judges, poring over the list.

Clint pulled his pen from his mouth and started to mark a couple of names on the sheet. "Some of these are dead, and I think he's in jail."

Pope tapped his list and smiled nostalgically. "Harry Newbold, god I loved him. I remember sleeping with Suzie Harker in the back of a seventy-one Austin Maxi listening to him, a voice like silk!"

"Dead!" announced Ricky curtly. "Pope, no harm to you, but I think most of the acts from your day would be on the do-not-resuscitate list. That's more like it, what about Jack Evans?"

Pope shook his head, a little embarrassed. "I don't know him, but I've got the internet wired up to the TV. Let's have a look."

"He was in one of the soaps," said Tom. "The women loved him. I think Mum had a soft spot for him as well."

Pope clicked a few buttons, and the video started playing. "Christ, that looks dated now!" said Clint. "But you're right, the women loved him."

Pope nodded his head in recognition. "He's a travel writer. It says here, looks like he's put on a little plumage over the years as well!"

"Stick him on the maybe list," suggested Ricky. "How many do we actually need?"

Tom looked at Clint for confirmation. "Seven or eight, I would have thought?"

Clint thought for a moment. "If we're doing one day only, I would say six acts. If we're going to do two days, we'd need more, but that would of course cost a lot more. I'm not sure doing two days would make sense financially?"

Tom nodded, and looked at Pope and Ricky. "Shall we do one day?"

"I would," said Ricky. "Two days, and the place will be destroyed."

Pope nodded. "It's a good point, and I don't think the villagers would be too impressed with a load of pissheads kicking around for two days!"

Tom clapped his hands together. "Great! So, one day it is, six acts spaced throughout the day. We need something else to break it up: a fairground, people juggling, cutting through ice with a chainsaw, blowing fire, that kind of shit!" Tom's mind was racing with ideas, and it felt great to share them with the others.

"What about a few amateur bands. You know, to break it up a bit?" suggested Ricky.

"Great idea!" agreed Clint. "We can get a battle of the bands going, and the best thing with amateurs is that they'll be free. They'll just be buzzing to play in front of a few hundred people."

Ricky continued scanning through the list. "Jesus, Kit Craig! We need him, he's nuts!"

Pope put the name into the computer and looked shocked. "No we don't, Ricky!"

Clint agreed with Pope. "We could probably do with a mix. Maybe a female singer, and if we can swing it, maybe a band."

The morning went quickly, and they were soon interrupted by people knocking on the door looking for their lunchtime pint.

Tom had been impressed by the collaborative approach and the sensible decisions that had been reached without conflict or arguing, despite the stakes being high for all involved. Some of the choices had been questionable, but in the end, all agreed on the final list, subject to availability cost.

Tom stood up, clutching a piece of paper containing six names: the names they had agonised over all morning, and more importantly, the names that were going to make them a lot of cash.

"So, after great deliberation, we have reached a decision. Our one-hit wonders are Jack Evans, The Supersonic Liberties, Hal Hogan, Laura Devine, Tommy Hake, and Karen Klein. And of course our very own Clint Lee!"

"Do you think they'll get offended by us calling them one-hit wonders?" asked Ricky. "I mean, it's not exactly complimentary."

"Nah," said Tom. "They'll just be glad of the phone call."

Clint was pleased that they had a list to work from. He was confident that most of the selection would be available and willing, but he had a couple of reserve names in case it didn't work out as planned. He stood up and shook hands with everyone, taking the list of names from Tom. "I need to go, gents. Leave this list with me and I'll see what I can do. How about I give you a call next week to let you know how things are going? Oh, what about cash, are we still going to offer them three K each?"

Tom looked at the group, who were nodding in agreement. "Yeah, three K. That should be more than enough. Cash on the day, though. I'm not paying anything upfront, in case they don't show."

Clint looked concerned. "I agree, but we need to give them something upfront, even if it's five hundred to secure the booking."

"Okay, five hundred pounds, and the rest on the day. If they have a website, ask them if we can stick a flyer for the festival on it, asked Tom. "Clint, getting these names is the most important bit. Once we have confirmation, we can start advertising and selling tickets. So if you can make it a priority that'd be great, mate."

"Of course, I'll be in touch soon!"

Tom had a sense of relief, a feeling that they were actually progressing. His only concern was that the group might endlessly discuss the idea without putting it into action. Pope was now busy serving the demanding lunchtime crowd, and Tom briefly considered a pint, but the remnants of his hangover suggested otherwise. *A bit of fresh air,* he thought.

Tom and Ricky took the short walk to the campsite, and Tom felt a little dejected looking at the lonely expanse of grass that was filled with tents only a few short weeks ago. A cold and long winter was not a major selling point for a campsite, and Tom knew it. Empty grass meant no money coming in, and whilst he was confident the festival would make money, he knew it would be foolish to rely on that as his only source of revenue.

He had arranged to spend the weekend with Carol, and while he wasn't looking forward to the drive, he couldn't wait to see her. Mike was out of the hospital, and reported that Carol was "killing him with kindness." Tom smiled when he heard this, because Mike could be in no better hands. They were speaking on the phone regularly, but Tom was desperate to spend more time with her. He enjoyed the flexibility of his job, which allowed him the time to spend with Carol, particularly with the distance currently between them.

Mike and Carol were eager to get involved with the organisation of the festival. Mike was still on leave from work, and he had no intention of returning. He had used his time to work out a business plan and a full costing breakdown, and with this information Tom now knew exactly how many tickets he needed to sell to make a profit. Whilst it was daunting, it seemed very achievable. Carol drew upon her years in advertising to draft ideas to promote the festival, and Tom was grateful for this help. With Clint working on the acts and the stage, and Pope sorting out the licence and stalls, it felt organised and in control. Tom and Ricky had assumed responsibility for everything else, and between them, Tom felt confident that they could make good money.

The ageing security guard stood with his arms folded, looking intently at the throbbing crowd stood before him. The crowd was a little more sedate than he was used to, but still an impressive turnout. He arched his neck, trying to locate the end of the queue, but it stretched out of the shop and disappeared down the street. The early arrivals had been in the shop for hours to ensure their place, and were now becoming a little agitated by the delay. A plump lady near the front of the line caught the eye of the security guard and impatiently tapped her watch, but was met with a shrug of the shoulders. The security guard looked over his shoulder toward the shop manager and gave a look that was not lost in translation.

He walked to the back of the shop and firmly opened the door marked 'staff only,' and protested: "We have to go, Una. They're getting impatient. We're an hour late, I need them to start buying books now so we can get through the queue!"

Clint sat on the corner of a desk, gripping onto his suit jacket to avoid it getting creased. He was frustrated at the delay, but Una had been on her phone virtually from the moment they'd arrived through the rear of the shop.

Una threw the shop manager a look that made Clint cringe; it was that look you give to a dog that shits on your new carpet. She placed her mobile phone carefully inside her elegant suit jacket. "A queue creates a queue," she said firmly.

The shop manager recoiled slightly and looked at Clint with a confused expression. Clint knew not to get involved, and paid sudden attention to the stitching on his newly tailored suit.

Una looked over. "Charlie, I have never let you down once, and I am not going to start today." She walked toward him and placed a reassuring hand on his shoulder. "If we make money, you make money. I am not going to jeopardise that. By keeping the people waiting, more and more people wander past and wonder what they're missing out on. Half the people in that queue will only be waiting because they saw the queue in the first place."

She looked at her watch and motioned toward Clint to follow her out of the small back office. She opened the door, and Clint was staggered by the number of people waiting for him. Once again, he'd doubted Una's methods, and once again, she'd proved why she was worth twenty percent.

Clint smiled, and waved nervously at the crowd before being ushered to his seat by the relieved security guard. It was surreal, as just a few months before, none of these people would have given him a second glance. Now they were queuing for hours just to see him and sign a book. He was still the same person as he was, which made him realise how fickle fame truly was, but he was more than happy to go along for the ride.

Surrounding Clint was a seemingly endless pile of books, along with a large banner with the words he'd been dreaming of: 'Number One Bestseller.'

Una nodded toward the security guard, who removed the symbolic velvet rope, and the first of the crowd moved toward Clint. The audience was a little more mature than it had once been, but Clint mopped up the adoration, happily posing for photographs, and listening to the anecdotes that people had obviously been rehearsing all day.

Una became a little frustrated, and made it clear to Clint that he needed to hurry up and move through the queue of people quicker. He didn't want to upset anybody, but he knew she was right — the purpose of the day was to sell more books.

The initial excitement soon wore off for Clint, as he took an exhausted look at the seemingly endless line of people. He had made the mistake of expressing a preference for Bourbon biscuits in a recent newspaper interview. He wasn't particularly keen on them, but the interviewer had asked him what his favourite biscuits were, and that was the first one he could think of. People were handing him packets of biscuits and expecting a reaction like they were the first person to do it. It was a novelty for Clint the first dozen times, but was becoming more and more frustrating, although he did appreciate the sentiment.

The allotted time for the book signing had come and gone, but the store manager had made a plea to Una to stay longer to work through the remaining people. He must have caught her at a weak moment, as she agreed without a request for further payment. Clint was now more relaxed, and enjoying the attention, smiling and posing for photographs when he needed to.

He looked at Una, who was again talking into her phone, and whilst he still wanted to punch her, he was grateful for what she'd done for him. He was also acutely aware that she could take it away from him as well.

His diary had been full for what seemed like weeks. The reception from his last TV appearance had been warm, and Una had been inundated with offers of work, helped also by the book jumping to the number one slot.

Clint was relieved to see the security guard close the door over and usher the last of the punters through it.

The store manager brought him a welcome cup of tea. Clint looked toward the large pile at his feet. "Biscuit, anyone?"

The store manager had a delighted grin across his face. "That is one of the best signings we've had this year. There was more at this than there was for Barlow!"

Una smiled, and impatiently ushered Clint toward the rear exit of the shop. Clint looked frustrated, and took one sip of his tea before removing his jacket from the rear of his chair. "Thanks, guys, great day!"

Una wasn't one for small talk, which sometimes was a blessing: it meant you could leave quickly, and blame her as the one being rude. "I'll give you a lift home," she said.

Clint didn't say anything, but he knew this was progress. He would never be friends with Una, but he was keen to break through the ice maiden persona that she so relished. He deliberately kept the conversation professional, as he had a chance of exuding a response. If Una didn't like the question, she wouldn't attempt a reply. She would simply ignore the question.

Clint waited for an opportune moment. "I need your help with something." He smiled because Una didn't even react or move her head. "I need you to help me get some acts for this festival I'm involved with. The charity festival."

Una cast a glance toward him. "It might be charity to you, but my twenty percent isn't going to charity."

Clint rolled his eyes, as he'd assumed Una wouldn't press for her cut, on the basis that his money was going to charity. He was acutely aware that their agreement meant she would get twenty percent off any deal he made, and to be fair, it was his fault that he'd committed to do this for charity. It now meant he had to give over money that was probably going to come out of his pocket. He knew it was his own fault, and quickly resigned himself to that fact.

"Who do you want, and how much do you want to pay?" asked Una. He ran through the list, and Una looked a little surprised at some of the choices, but shrugged her shoulders. "That's fine, consider it done. I'll get the girls in the office to make the bookings tomorrow."

Clint was impressed with Una and the way she handled things. She didn't muck around. She just made things happen. "You are really pulling out the big guns for this one, aren't you!" she added sarcastically. He expected this type of reaction, which was the reason he was hesitant to ask in the first place. Una sensed that she had hurt his feelings. "Look, I don't want you to fail. This could be good for your image, if you do it right! But you aren't going to sell shit with that line-up!"

Deep down, he knew she was right. It would be great for his profile, which was why he wanted it to be a success. Plus, he'd started too really like Tom and the rest of the guys, which was further incentive to make a success of it.

Una paused for a moment. "How about I get you The Overview?"

Clint looked at Una and smiled. "Are you being serious?"

"I don't joke where business is concerned. Do you want me to get them for you or not?"

Clint was staggered. "Of course I do. Shit, they could fill the event on their own. But how much are they going to cost?"

"Don't worry about the cost. It's on me. They owe me for sorting something out. The girls will make the arrangements tomorrow."

"I may be a bitch, but I look after the people I work with. As long as you make me money and don't fuck me over, I'll look out for you." She pulled the car to the side of the road. "Good work today, kid. Now get out!"

Clint considered leaning over to kiss her on the cheek, but quickly thought better of it. "Thanks, Una. I mean it!"

He watched as she sped away, and at that moment took time to reflect on the day. His book was a number one bestseller. 'A tale of a singer with moderate success who lost everything' was something people wanted to read? It was a concept that he couldn't quite rationalise, but one that overwhelmed him, and one he didn't want to question in great detail.

As he opened the post left at his front door, he smiled because the envelopes had fuelled his depression for months. Final demands and veiled threats served only to enhance the spiral of self-destruction. They now brought him a feeling of self-worth as he looked at the bank statement, which was larger than he'd ever imagined. Cheques and endorsements were flooding through, and were only likely to increase.

He'd heard stories of businessmen who'd only truly found success and wealth once they'd lost it all, once they'd been bankrupt. It was a concept he'd previously struggled with, but in that moment he was starting to truly understand it. He'd been at the lowest ebb, and through an element of self-determination and luck, had been able to turn a significant corner.

It was a clichéd feeling, but he felt like the shroud of failure had been lifted, and he could almost feel the hunger he felt when he was an aspiring musician. It was difficult for him to quantify, but he just knew he was on the cusp of turning his life around, and most importantly, shaking the reputation of being a loser.

He stood in the middle of his small, restrictive flat that had been his refuge for months, and looked with disdain at the depressing painted walls that served only to remind him of his recent past. He took another look at the bank statement in his hand. While they were only digits on paper, for him it meant the difference between escaping his past and distancing himself from his demons, a chance to truly make a new start.

"I am getting out of this dump!"

Chapter Seven

Tom gingerly pressed the keyboard on his laptop, almost afraid to hit the refresh button. It was a ritual that had now become daily at the very least.

Mike had become a party to this exercise, and sat staring intently at Tom, impatiently clicking a pen in his hand. Tom raised his head and deliberately delayed his response, increasing the tension but also the frustration for Mike.

Tom took a deep breath and paused for a moment longer. "One hundred and ten overnight!" he announced.

Mike lifted his head and smiled. "That's over four thousand now?"

Tom purposefully pressed the keys on the calculator, and confirmed Mikes understanding. "Sure is. One hundred and ten tickets in one night is the biggest jump we've had. Clint must have been on the TV or something for it to jump that much."

The ticket sales had been slow, and whilst he maintained a positive outward image, Tom had been concerned. They were approaching the break-even point, but ticket sales had continued to slow. Once the line-up had been confirmed, there was an initial flurry of sales, but that had long since petered off to a steady trickle. Clint was pushing the festival at every opportunity, and Tom was pleased he was involved, because without the publicity he was able to garner, ticket sales would have been in the hundreds rather than the thousands.

Carol walked nervously into the front room, trying to read the expression on the faces before her. "Well?"

"A little over four thousand," replied Tom. "Only about another three thousand to go!" he added with a tinge of frustration in his voice.

Carol walked toward him and placed a reassuring hand on his shoulder. "Still another six weeks to go!"

It didn't seem two minutes since there were three months to go, and that was causing Tom to panic. Mike could sense the anxiety in Tom's voice. "Even if you didn't sell another ticket you would have still covered your costs. Anything now is a bonus. Plus, don't forget what they'll spend on the day."

Tom was acutely aware of the break-even point, but too much effort had gone into organising the festival for them to simply walk away without making any money. He was also aware that Larry would be expecting cash at the end of this festival. After all, he'd kept to his side of the bargain, and Mike had received no further unwanted visits.

Larry had kept his distance, except for the occasional phone call to discuss progress. He had remained the consummate professional, and at no point had given Tom any cause for concern, but he felt indebted every time he phoned. It was a feeling that he didn't like.

Tom had enjoyed working with Carol. They'd become closer over the last few weeks, and the distance between them had not caused the problems he thought it would. If anything, it meant that each time they met felt like an event, something to look forward to. Ricky had now finished the cabins, which meant that Carol spent more time commuting from Manchester. But Tom also enjoyed spending time in the city, as it gave him the opportunity to hang out with Mike, who was now fully recovered, albeit still signed off from work.

While the physical scars were now almost fixed, Tom noticed that Mike was not quite the same, and felt like the accident had taken away some of his confidence. He had not mentioned this to Mike, but Carol had also noticed the subtle change. Mike was becoming a little reclusive, and days would pass without him leaving the house. Despite their best efforts to coax him out for an evening, Mike would find a reason to remain at home.

"We need a final push on these tickets," said Tom enthusiastically.

"We do," said Carol. "But without sounding negative, we've done everything. We've done social media, but without a big advertising budget, our options are limited."

"I know, and you've both done an amazing job!"

Tom was conscious that Carol and Mike had given up a lot of time to help with the marketing and logistics, and didn't want to sound like he wasn't grateful.

"If we've done what we can, then we need to engage people who can help us give this a major push!" said Tom.

"Like who?" asked Mike.

"Like Clint and Larry. Think about it. They've got as much invested in this as I have, but they're not exactly losing sleep over it. If Larry wants to get paid, he must know people who can get the word out, and Clint, well, what's he really done? Okay, he's mentioned the festival when asked, but he promised a load of cash to charity, and if tickets sales don't ramp up then he'll look like a prize twat. I need to get them more on board. At the minute, Larry is going to get twenty percent of nothing, and I'm sure he doesn't want that."

"Yeah, but Larry?" asked Mike. "Do you really want to get any more involved with him?"

"No, but I think I need him. He knows everyone. He'd always been fine with me, and he's good at what he does. Just ask your *friend*!"

Mike looked a little sheepish, and was extremely grateful for Larry's intervention. He was also very aware that Tom was only involved with Larry as a favour to him.

"Plus, Clint is everywhere at the minute," added Tom. "He's in the papers all the time, and always on the TV. He must be able to push it a bit more."

"Surely he can push the charity side of things?" suggested Carol.

"I just need to get this event back onto his radar," said Tom. "Make this a priority for him. I know he's busy, but this needs a bit of his focus. Plus he's got twenty K invested, and no matter how much work he's got on, he won't want to lose any of that."

"Tell him that Larry is coming after him!" Carol joked.

"I might just do that," replied Tom. "I really need this to work out. The campsite is dead. I knew it was going to be quiet once the summer was over, but Christ, I didn't realise how bad it was going to be."

"If you need any cash, mate, just let me know," said Mike.

"Thanks, but I'm fine. You know me, I can survive on nothing, but it's been nice having a few quid in my pocket. I just need to make the money we take in the summer last throughout the winter. Or make a few quid on events like this, which will bankroll us through the quiet spells. We're starting to get a few bookings in for the summer, which helps. Plus, I've got a really wealthy girlfriend, which helps!"

"Girlfriend!" teased Carol.

Tom smiled because it had occurred to him that they had never had a conversation to discuss the status of their relationship. They were spending more and more time together, and Tom felt really comfortable in her company. She was his girlfriend, although he had never officially announced it.

"Well the job's yours if you want it!" said Tom. "I'm holding interviews for the position a little later on!"

"On that bombshell, I think I'll leave you two lovebirds to it," said Mike. "Try and keep the interview noise down, though!"

Carol poured a glass of wine and cuddled into Tom. "It sounded nice, to hear you call me your girlfriend. I could get used to it. Does this mean I can now introduce you to people as my boyfriend?"

"Of course! It's one of the perks of the job. I know I joke Carol, but you and me... it's nice. I'm enjoying it. You know I'm not good at this sort of stuff, so I want you to know I like you. Really like you."

Carol smiled again because she knew how bad Tom was at expressing anything remotely romantic, so for him to have said that, he must have really meant it.

"I like you as well. You're really dreamy!" she said with a laugh. "Maybe you can hold my hand next time we go out?"

"Steady!" replied Tom. "One small step at a time." Tom didn't like to hold hands, and Carol knew this, purposefully grabbing his hand at every opportune moment. "It isn't just the cash, you know," he said. "The festival, the campsite, and all that. I like the money, but it's more than that. I want a future, hopefully one with you in it?"

"I know, and I'm really proud of you, Tom. Look how much you've done in the last year. Thank you for helping Mike out with that situation as well. I know you've had to give up a lot, but I couldn't bear it if anything happened to him."

"I know. I love the nerd as well. Just don't tell him I said that!"

"Do you think about Larry and that bloke that ran Mike over?"

"No. Well, I try not to, but it had crossed my mind."

"What do you think happened to him? Do you think Larry would have hurt him?"

"I doubt it. Besides, he wouldn't have done anything himself. He would have paid someone to do it for him. Larry isn't stupid. He wouldn't get involved in something that would get him in trouble. He probably just had the guy taken to one side and gently asked him to not bother Mike anymore."

"'Gently' is probably not the word I would have used," added Carol.

"I don't feel guilty, to be honest," said Tom. "Yes, Mike was bang out of order by shagging his wife, but nearly killing a man in broad daylight? That is well and truly over the top.

Mike hasn't heard from him again, so hopefully that's the end of that. I just have to make sure I have a large envelope I can give to Larry, as I don't fancy telling him there's no cash."

"You're going to sell thousands more tickets, so you can give Larry his cash and we can put all of this stuff behind us. My dreamboat boyfriend the music promoter… all the girls in the hospital will be jealous. When you make your fortune, you can take us both away, somewhere nice. Somewhere with a private balcony where we can sit naked, drinking wine and watching the sunset!"

"Now that sounds like a plan!" said Tom, raising his glass.

Tom cuddled into Carol, and remembered the times he'd looked at her from afar, desperately wondering what it would be like to be with her. Their relationship was still in its infancy, but it felt right, it felt like everything he'd imagined. He didn't want Carol to think that he was motivated only by money, and in truth, as long as he had a pound more than he could spend, he was happy. He was beginning to feel the pressure of responsibility, a responsibility to Pope, to Ricky, to his mum, to Larry, and most importantly, to Carol. He was weighed down by the fear of failure, and wondered if his previous life, one lead with nonchalance, was a defence mechanism. He'd now put his head firmly above the parapet, and whilst the promise of success was a strong aphrodisiac, the fear of failure would have been terminal. He was concerned that if the festival were a commercial failure, he'd regress to a life he was trying so desperately to escape — a life without responsibility or a future, but most importantly, a life without Carol. He enjoyed the respect that came with responsibility, and was desperate to avoid anything that would be a challenge to his new life, even if that challenge was failure itself.

The alarm startled Carol, who rolled over, expecting Tom to press the snooze button. The alarm continued, and with bleary eyes, Carol reached for the clock. Tom was never an early riser, so his absence had surprised Carol. She smiled as she picked up a napkin from his pillow with a message drawn in her lipstick. Her first thought was that the message looked vaguely sinister written in bright red lipstick: 'Gone to see Clint, will bring back breakfast X.'

Tom was concerned at his reliance on Clint, who was becoming increasingly difficult to contact. He had no doubt that he'd deliver what he'd promised, but Tom had a nagging concern that was difficult to shake. Clint had publicly committed to the event, but Tom knew that neither he nor the event was a priority for Clint. Clint was the key to the publicity, and had access to the acts, so Tom was very aware that he had to keep the lines of communication open. Carol was keen to give Clint a second chance, but had harboured the same concerns, a concern that the renewed fame would ultimately lead him down that same path of self-destruction he had walked before.

Tom walked up the secluded cul-de-sac to Clint's new home. He knew Clint was making money, but the size of the property and the location took him by surprise. The townhouse was on a newly built development with a central gated communal park area. The value of the cars that adorned the properties confirmed his assumption of an exorbitant purchase price. He was impressed, and whilst he loved the country, this suited him. He momentarily imagined his life surrounded by such opulence in this oasis, moments from the hustle of the city. He cautiously approached the townhouse, checking to make sure he was at the correct property before knocking on the door. There was no sign of movement, but he had too much riding on Clint, and would have waited on the doorstep if necessary. The door eventually opened, and Clint nodded in acknowledgement before gesturing for Tom to come in.

One look at Clint, and Tom could tell he'd been drinking, and judging by the smell and appearance, it had been over a number of days. The house was impressive, but showed the characteristic hallmarks of someone battling a serious drinking problem. The living room was strewn with empty beer cans and wine bottles, and there was a choking layer of cigarette smoke hanging in the room. Tom knew immediately that his worse fears had been confirmed: Clint was a mess.

The old-looking man sat in a distinguished leather Sherlock chair under the main front window, his head now buried in his hands. Tom was taken aback by the appearance of this celebrity who had presented himself so immaculately during their recent meetings. He was unsure if Clint was at the start of a drinking session or had reached the end of one, but either way, he knew he was in trouble. This drunken mess slumped before him was due to headline his fledgling music festival in a few short weeks. Tom was reliant on this man to deliver the acts that had been promised to all the people who'd bought tickets. He was concerned for himself and Ricky, but more than that, he'd got Pope involved, and then he thought about Larry, before he also slumped his head in his hands. The two sat quietly, and Tom was unsure if Clint had fallen asleep.

He composed himself and took a deep breath. "What the fuck, Clint?" Clint barely acknowledged him, and reached for a can that wasn't covered in discarded cigarette butts. "Clint, you are a mess!"

Tom shook his head and paced around the living room. He'd been around enough drunken people over the years to recognise when someone was too wasted to listen. In any other circumstance, he would have left Clint to wallow in his own drunken self-pity, but his short-term future was at stake.

"Clint, you need to listen to me. I need the phone numbers for the acts you've booked."

Clint looked up momentarily, and gave a sarcastic smile, motioning his hand in a gestured dismissal. Tom knew it was useless, but he reminded Clint of the money he'd invested in the festival, and told him that if the festival didn't go ahead, Clint would lose all of his money.

Clint momentarily looked up, and beneath the scruffy stubble Tom could see an evil streak in him. Carol had told him that Clint was a nasty drunk, and he could now see this for himself. Clint shook his head and smiled briefly. "How much, twenty K?" Clint started to laugh.

Tom was getting frustrated, but had to stay cautious, as he was unsure what Clint was capable of when drunk.

Clint fumbled for a cigarette, almost falling from his seat. The motion knocked the can, and lager spilt onto the freshly-laid cream carpet, which was peppered with cigarette burns. "I gambled twenty K yesterday," he mumbled, "and will probably do the same today."

It was clear that Clint was a liability. Tom didn't know what he was going to do, but he knew it couldn't involve Clint. He stood up and looked at Clint with disgust. "You're a disgrace, a washed-up loser. What is worse, Clint, people took a chance on you. Carol told me what a wanker you were, but even she was prepared to give you a chance, and you have thrown it back. You don't deserve another chance. Go for a shower. You stink."

Tom turned his back on Clint, and walked toward the door, desperate to escape the acrid plume of stale nicotine and despair.

"I will give you the numbers. Well, I will get Una to give you the numbers." Tom paused, and turned around, looking at Clint to see if he was being serious. "I want Carol," he added.

Tom looked confused. "What do you mean you want Carol?"

Clint leaned forward and stared intently. "I want you to disappear, and I want Carol back!"

Tom felt a little intimidated, but hid it well. "Look at yourself, son, you're a mess. Do you think Carol would go anywhere near you? We're finished. I don't want to see you again. I will phone Una direct." Tom didn't look back and headed for the door. "What a wanker!" he muttered to himself.

He was shocked at how the alcohol had affected Clint's appearance, but how it had also affected his personality. He took a lungful of fresh air and grimaced at the stale aroma that had attached itself to his clothing. Meeting Clint in that state was surreal, and Tom was glad to be rid of him. He knew that Clint was a big name, and people who'd bought tickets would be disappointed. Clint was on a road to ruin, and Tom distancing himself from him was probably not a bad thing.

As Tom walked home, he thought about Clint wanting to get back with Carol. Was this a chance remark said in a drunken stupor, or something more serious? He knew that Carol wouldn't get back with Clint, but it didn't stop him panicking at the thought.

He smiled to himself as he wondered what the hell he'd got himself involved with. Yes he'd wanted to do something different with his life, but how had he got involved with an idiot like Clint and a headcase like Larry? He thought about the worst-case scenario. What if he just pulled the plug now and walked away? As tempting as it was, he'd already spent too much money, and besides, Larry would still want something for the work he'd done. Plus, Pope had trusted him with his money. It wasn't ideal, but the control was now back with him. He didn't have to worry about Clint, or sit waiting for the phone to ring.

Tom fulfilled his promise, and brought breakfast back for Carol and Mike, before explaining the meeting he'd just had with Clint. It was difficult for him to explain just how bad Clint looked, but Carol reminded him that she'd seen it all before.

"Did he have that evil, drunken look?" she asked.

Tom sympathised with what Carol must have gone through with Clint previously. "He said he wants to get back with you."

Carol laughed and looked almost a little repulsed. "He has phoned me a couple of times this week," she confessed. "When he was drunk. I told him where to go, and not to phone me anymore."

Tom didn't see Clint as a real threat, but he was relieved to hear Carol confirm it. "Let me know if he calls again?" he asked.

"Did you get the numbers of the acts from him?" asked Mike.

"No, I need to speak to his agent, Una, and hope she'll hand them over. I get the impression that it's going to cost me money to get them, though!"

"We need to hope that Clint has actually paid them the deposits in the first place," said Mike.

"Shit, I didn't even think about that," replied Tom. "What if he hasn't?"

"If he hasn't, you've sold thousands of tickets to a festival with no music."

Tom looked at Carol and laughed ironically. "Clint has dropped me right in it!"

Una took her usual seat under the arch, facing the window, but with her back to the wall. She enjoyed the view, but purposefully chose that seat so that the arch would separate her from the neighbouring tables. Those close to Una joked that she was a recluse, but the truth was she enjoyed her own company. The staff at the intimate coffee shop close to her offices would deliberately try to engage her in polite conversation to see who could evoke a meaningful reply. Most had failed. Una was never rude, but her matter-of-fact candid approach meant that she would appear curt and unapproachable. She knew this, and often played on it, using it as an ideal opportunity to avoid small talk and other distractions.

A petite, smartly dressed waitress approached Una and took her order, as well as the opportunity to exchange pleasantries. Una smiled but didn't respond, instead returning to her blackberry, which she valued as much as a gunslinger valued a Colt .45. The girls in the coffee shop knew Una well, and didn't take offence. She was blunt when she wanted to be, but remained courteous to the man on the street. To those in the profession, she could be formidable, and her vicious tongue was legendary.

She could see someone approach her table, but didn't break her gaze from her phone. Assuming it was her coffee, she reached for her purse, but was startled as an older gentleman sat opposite her with a broad smile on his face. She looked around, confused, desperately trying to recognise the face. She had dealt with a large number of people, and assumed this was a contact she couldn't recall.

The man was smartly dressed in an expensive black suit, with a starched white shirt with the top button open. He had broad shoulders, and although his features were rugged, there was a kind face, but one that Una was struggling to place.

The man before her said nothing, and stirred his coffee. Was he just sharing the table? Una looked around, and there were plenty of empty tables, so why had he chosen this one?

The waitress returned with her coffee, and placed it on the table. The man slowly leaned forward, and using his spoon, began to stir her coffee. Una was unsure what was happening, and a wave of panic shot through her before she broke the silence. "What are you doing?" she asked calmly. She was unsure if this was a business associate or a deranged stalker. Either way, she wanted to remain calm and avoid any provocation.

The man put the spoon on the table and politely offered Una a pot of sugar, which she declined. He looked up and stared intently with warm blue eyes and a purposeful smile. To the staff of the coffee shop they must have appeared as old friends, possibly more.

The man finally spoke in a gentle but gruff voice. "Your boy owes me sixty K."

Una looked blankly at him, her mind racing, trying to understand what he was referring to. She stuttered her words, losing her famously cold persona. "Who? What sixty K?"

"Your boy, Clint Lee. He owes me sixty K."

Una sat back in her chair, trying to digest his words. "My boy?"

"Yes, your boy. Your boy, Clint, has had a bit of a losing streak, and owes me sixty K."

Una had not spoken to Clint for a while, and their relationship had soured somewhat, as Una was unable to secure the stage work Clint had been hoping for. He was earning money for Una, but was by no means a big client, so she'd distanced herself from him. She'd heard stories from friends in the press that he was drinking again, but she didn't need the grief.

Composing herself, she said, "I'm sorry to hear he owes you money, but I'm not sure what that has to do with me?"

"You are his agent. You control the purse strings. Now, the truth is, I've been around to see him to ask for my cash, but he is in a bit of mess, drinking and who-knows-what-else. Now, I see this guy on TV all the time. My son even bought me his book, which I thought was a touch ironic."

The waitress briefly interrupted them by asking if they wanted anything else. The man politely declined on behalf of them both.

"It was poor, you know, the book. I should ask you for a refund." The man paused, waiting for a reaction but Una sat almost frozen. "I'm just kidding, about the refund. Anyway, I digress. My apologies. Your boy owes me a large chunk of change, and looking at him, I'm starting to doubt that he's going to pay up."

"I understand he owes you money," said Una, "but I still don't understand why you're telling me. If he owes you money, then that is his problem. I don't even like the man. You need to speak with *him*."

The man took a sip of his coffee, deliberately taking his time. "I understand, Una, and he is quite an odious little chap, isn't he? The problem I have is that I am owed a lot of money, and the only way he's going to get it to me is if he works. Now, Clint has told me that you're his agent, so logically you are the person who can get him work. If he works, then he can get me my money. Plus, any money he makes would filter through you, would it not?"

Una nodded. "Yes, but if he's drinking, there's nothing I can do for him. No one will give him any work."

"I hear you are the best in the business, Una, you *can* get him to work if you try hard enough, and when he does, I want you to pay the money till he covers what he owes me. Fair enough?"

Una was now a little frustrated. "No, not fair enough! Take it up with Clint yourself. Now please excuse me, I have an appointment."

She stood up to leave as the man calmly placed a white envelope on the table. She looked at him, unsure what she was to do with the envelope. The man gestured her to open it. She picked it up, and slowly opened it until she could see its contents. She sat down slowly, and felt the blood drain from her face.

The man smiled and took another drink from his coffee. "All I want is the sixty K that Clint owes me, nothing more. Once I get that, you will not hear from me again. Can I assume that we are clear on this? I want the sixty K in the next month. How you choose to arrange that with Clint is up to you, but either way, I get the money."

Una looked resigned and nodded her head. "You'll get your money."

The man stood up and smiled. "It was nice to meet you, Una." He slowly walked away from the table before pausing. "I must apologise for being so rude. I didn't introduce myself. My name is Larry."

Una watched Larry leave the coffee shop, and took a deep breath. The young waitress could see that she was distressed, and asked if she could get her anything. Una was grateful, and in a moment of vulnerability, lost her cold persona.

She collected her thoughts for a few moments before taking a short walk back to her office. Larry had not been aggressive, but she felt nervous, looking over her shoulder, conscious of those around her. She considered phoning the police, because ultimately what Larry was doing was blackmail. She quickly dismissed any such thoughts, as she knew if the contents of that envelope got out, it would cost her a lot more than sixty thousand pounds.

Although Clint had not been working for a while, he was still marketable, and if she could keep his drinking out of the press, there was still scope to get him work. She would be damned if she was going to pay the money to Larry.

She made a call to the journalist who had tipped her off about Clint drinking again. He was happy to keep the stories under wraps, because a favour owed from Una was worth considerably more than a small story that would appear in the gossip section of the newspaper. Having Una in your corner was gold dust for a journalist, as she not only knew the stories, she created most of them.

She desperately tried to contact Clint, without success. With hindsight, this was something of a relief. She was furious with him, and her anger would have made her irrational and unfocused. She looked through her records to see how many outstanding invoices she owed to Clint, but it was well short of what she owed to Larry.

Una didn't like Clint, a fact she had made clear to him on previous occasions, and after the reports of his drinking, she'd reached the decision to sever all ties with him. Now she would have to place those plans on hold, at least until Larry was paid off.

Tom walked up the steep steps, which were adorned with pictures of celebrities and a lady who he assumed was Una. He smiled as he saw a picture of Clint, which was obviously taken in the infancy of his career. He was nervous as he walked through the reception door, as he knew that Una was pretty much the last hope he would have of making the festival a success.

He walked toward the pretty receptionist and asked if he could speak to Una. The receptionist took his details and asked him to take a seat.

"Una, I'm sorry to bother you, but I have Tom in reception for you. He said it relates to a music gig Clint Lee was working on with him?"

Una smiled. "Jesus, considering I don't want anything to do with that arsehole, he sure is popular today! What does he want with me?"

"I don't know, Una, he said he wanted to speak with you. Do you want me to tell him you're busy?"

"No, send him in. Hopefully he owes Clint some money."

Tom sat down in front of Una, who was distinctly frosty toward him. "You want to talk to me about Clint Lee?" she said firmly.

Tom was a little taken aback by her abruptness, and struggled to articulate what he'd rehearsed several times during the night. "Clint has let me down, and I was hoping you could help me?"

"You and me both, honey, you and me both!"

He explained to her the state he'd found Clint in, and how he had failed to deliver the acts as promised. Una was initially confused about the relationship between Clint and the festival, until she recalled the ridiculous pledge to donate his proceeds to charity.

"So what acts did he promise you?" she asked.

Tom ran through the list of the acts they had advertised, and explained how he'd given Clint a deposit to secure the bookings. Una didn't need this today, but she quickly realised that any profit Clint might make from this concert would partly filter down to her, so she was happy to listen to the full story.

"Clint was going to appear as well, which was a big draw when it came to selling the tickets. Clint also promised us The Overview."

"How many tickets have you sold?

"Well, that was the problem. We've been doing our own advertising. Clint was supposed to be plugging it, but he'd been on the piss instead, so we've only sold just over four thousand tickets."

"How much was Clint due to get from this?"

"Thirty percent. But he allocated that to charity."

"Honey, Clint is no longer involved in this, so his thirty percent comes to me, and after any expenses, if there's anything left, I will square Clint away."

Tom was more than happy with that, and didn't care if Clint didn't get a penny. Tom was also open with Una about the money they'd all put toward the festival. At this stage, the only money that had been handed over was the deposit to secure the acts, which Tom assumed Clint had now frittered away.

Una hammered some figures into her calculator, and soon realised that she could make some money from this, easily enough to pay back Larry and cover her expenses. Most of the hard work had been done, so she could make a lot of cash quickly and with minimum effort, bar a few phone calls.

She gave a list of the acts to her receptionist and asked her to tell them they were being booked to appear at the festival. "They're all clients, so there'll be no problem." She was also aware that she'd be making her agents fee from all of the acts booked, so Tom walking into her office could prove quite profitable for her.

"What about The Overview?" asked Tom. "Can we get them? They are pretty much the reason most people have bought tickets."

Like Tom, Una knew that they were the key to making any money out of this. The other acts had been commercially successful, but that was years ago. People wouldn't buy tickets solely to see them. "You'll need to leave that one with me," she said. "But work on the assumption that they'll be appearing."

The receptionist returned, and confirmed that none of the acts she'd spoken to had heard from Clint, and none of them had received any deposit to appear. Tom shook his head and realised the gravity of the situation. If he hadn't come to see Una, he would have lost everything. "The other thing, Una, is the ticket sales. Can you help us get some advertising? I know it's short notice, but if we don't sell the tickets, we don't make any money."

Una looked confused. "Yes, but I don't understand how you only sold four thousand tickets if you advertised that The Overview were appearing. That alone should have sold it out."

"I don't think people believed us. Let's face it, a band like that appearing at a debut festival, I didn't believe it myself, but Clint assured us it was nailed on."

"I need to think about this," said Una. "It's been a somewhat strange day. Leave your number with the girls, and I will call you, Tim."

"It's Tom. And thanks, Una. I mean it, I'd be well and truly screwed without you."

Una nodded, but didn't look up as Tom walked tentatively out of her office. She sat back in her chair, and kicked off her shoes as she shouted to Fiona, her receptionist, "Get me a meeting with the usual faces from the press!"

Fiona walked in, clutching her notepad. "No problem, Una. Shall I tell them what it's about?"

"Tell them that The Overview is making their comeback gig next month, and Fiona, get me Paul Yorke from The Overview on the phone. If he doesn't want to take the call, just tell him that I am one phone call away from ruining his career!"

"Joe, Fiona from Una Jacob's office on line one."

"Christ. Okay, thanks, Emma. Fiona, this is a rare and unexpected pleasure, what does our despotic Una want with the leading newspaper on Fleet Street?"

Fiona laughed. "That is pretty much the same response I've had from my previous five phone calls!"

"What, you mean I wasn't the first person you called? I'm deeply hurt!"

"Joe, all of you showbiz journalists have thick hides. It must be a survival instinct built into all parasites, you know, like cockroaches."

"Even cockroaches have feelings, you know! Anyway, enough of this pillow talk. What's up?"

"Press release coming over to you as we speak. Check your inbox."

"Coming through," said Joe, opening the attachment. "The Overview. I thought them boys were finished. Where the fuck is this they are playing? I thought they were taking an extended break due to Yorke having a bit of an affliction with the old Colombian talcum powder?"

"You are the journalist, Joe. Anyway, must go! Plenty more of Fleet Street's finest to talk to!"

"What was that about?" asked Emma, who had been desperately trying to listen in to the conversation.

"The Overview is making a comeback next month at some amateur-time festival with a load of D-list acts."

"Ooh, I like them, but I thought they were calling it a day?"

"They were taking an extended break, because Paul Yorke was a cokehead, apparently. But why would they appear in some backwater with a load of has-beens? I don't get it. Plus Una Jacob is involved. There is something definitely not right."

"So, are you going to run with the story?"

"Absolutely. They are big news. Plus, me and you can have a little trip out to the country if we can find this place. In all the time I have done this job, Una Jacob has never given out a press release. She must be desperate for this to work out. If I run this, she'll owe me a little favour, and Una Jacob is a great person to owe you a favour!"

"Emma, have a phone around your contacts at the other papers. See what they know? If we work quickly on this, we might get it on the front page."

Fiona walked into Una's office, and placed a coffee on her desk. "I have called the papers, and they seemed keen. Paul

Yorke wasn't on that number we had, but I have a mobile number for you."

Una smiled and nodded her head, reaching out for the number. "Let's see if we can put a music festival on."

It had been a few weeks since Una had last spoken to Paul Yorke. Her contacts in the press were giving her more reports that Paul and other band members were dabbling in more than alcohol, and were becoming a liability for Una, failing to show up on numerous occasions. The Overview were one of her biggest clients, and she had been their agent from the beginning, but having an unreliable client reflected badly on her. Despite the healthy commission they made her, she would not jeopardise her business for one client. This was their last chance with Una, who had already decided to cut them loose.

"Paul, this is Una."

The phone went quiet, almost as if a small child was desperately trying to think of an excuse for being absent from school. "Una, hi, it's good to hear from you."

Paul grimaced, and put the phone on his chest. He felt guilty for the way he'd behaved toward Una, who had supported him personally since day one. He had tried desperately to get a contract, and Una took a chance on him. He didn't want to let her down, but he was becoming tired of dealing with the same people, day in day out.

"You guys have let me down, big time," said Una, "but that is a conversation for another day. You guys are on your last legs. I have got you an intimate gig for next month doing a debut music festival."

Paul was confused. People had told him they had heard about some music festival promoting The Overview as being their lead act. He had assumed it was someone using their name to sell tickets and then offer a lame apology when they failed to show up.

"No offence, Una, but I am not doing some gig in the arsehole of nowhere."

Una shook her head, having already assumed this was the reaction she would get. A few months before, she would have done anything for Paul, as he was making her a fortune, but since they had dropped off the scene, her cheques had dried up. She knew that if they continued on the same path they were on, they'd be finished, so she was in a no-lose situation.

"Look, Paul, you're doing this. I had an interesting conversation with some head case called Larry today. He showed me some interesting still photographs of a video you're in. I could also see that arsehole Clint Lee in the pictures."

Paul went quiet, desperately racking his brains to recall the video in question. In truth, the last few months had been a blur. He had known Clint years before, but had lost touch when Clint's career took a nosedive. They had met again at a music award show, and often ended up wasted at the same parties. It was at these parties that Clint succumbed to the demons he had eluded for so long.

"I assume from your silence you have no idea what I'm talking about?" added Una.

"No, no I don't," was the hushed response.

Una smiled. She had correctly assumed that Paul would have no recollection. "You are in a video snorting allsorts, naked with a load of whores. Paul, some of those girls looked underage!"

It was true that Paul was in a video naked, and there were presumably prostitutes, but none of them were underage. Una knew that Paul wouldn't care less if people saw him snorting cocaine off the naked bodies of prostitutes. If anything, he would have been quite proud. But she knew he would be devastated if he thought they were underage. She was unsure whether she wanted to use this tactic, which was abhorrent even by her own standards, but she needed leverage to get both him and his career back on track. Once he was back in line, she would simply say that she had found the girls in question, and he would be pleased to know that they were in fact older than they looked.

Paul felt physically sick. He had a vague recollection of being with Clint and a load of girls, but the night was a drug and alcohol-induced blur. "I don't understand, Una, how is there a video, and who is Larry?"

Una knew she had Paul on the ropes, and whilst she didn't take much delight in it, she justified it to herself that she was doing this for his benefit. "Your friend, Clint, is a degenerate gambler who owes Larry a fortune. When Clint couldn't pay him what he owed, he must have shown Larry the video he'd recorded and hoped it would settle his debt if he sold it to the papers. That is not Larry's style, so he came to see me, as he knew I was your agent and Clint's. He knew this would end your career and therefore cost me money. All he is looking for is his cash."

Paul swore under his breath. "That piece of shit, Clint."

"That he is," replied Una. "He'd got involved in some concert he'd helped organise with a share going to charity. He thought it would help his career. Seemingly, he offered up your name on the bill in an attempt to sell tickets, which in truth failed miserably. So in an effort to get Larry paid off and save your ass, I have had to take over, and I need you and the band to appear at this concert next month. That way, Larry disappears from our life, and you don't end up in jail, but instead continue to make yourself, and me, lots of money."

"What if Larry continues to blackmail me?"

"That's what I thought," added Una. "But I have made a few calls today, and Larry is proper old-school, a man of his word. We have no choice but to assume that once I pay him his cash that Clint owes, we won't hear from him again. He assured me that Clint doesn't have any other copies."

Paul digested what Una had said, and she was right. He had little choice. He was ashamed and disgusted with himself. "Una, thank you. I know I've let you down, but I won't do it again. We'll be there, just let me know the details."

Chapter Eight

Soak it up, Ricky, absorb every moment of this, because it will disappear in an instant."

Tom stood with his arm around Ricky as they watched the giant stage being erected in the far corner of the campsite. A number of the villagers had joined them as they stood transfixed, as a small army of technicians brought order to a chaotic mass of cables and metal.

Tom felt emotional as he saw the physical representation of months of work slowly taking shape in front of him. He was under no illusion that in spite of the hard work, there was an element of luck and good fortune, and the key element, Una Jacob.

Una had been a revelation, and he was staggered at her ability to get things sorted with a simple phone call. It had been a learning curve for him, and a steep one that he'd shared with those closest to him. Una was aloof and blunt, but Tom soon realised that was just the way she worked. He could understand how people would see her as being rude and arrogant, but he looked beyond this, and just admired someone who was good at her craft.

A steady stream of intrigued journalists throughout the week had been a welcome distraction for Tom and Ricky, who were becoming minor celebrities in their own right, appearing in several publications. Tom was under no illusion that the attention was mostly due to The Overview making their comeback, but he didn't care why they were here, just the fact that they were!

The Overview had appeared on several primetime TV shows to announce their comeback, and once word had got out, ticket sales exploded. Tom had struggled to comprehend how quickly the tickets had sold out, with tickets selling by the hundreds every time he clicked the refresh button on his computer. The money from these sales had been flooding in, along with several other deals that Una had secured, such as sponsorship of the event, and TV coverage to air the highlights. It was beyond anything that Tom had imagined at the beginning when they'd first started working on the idea, but Carol kept his feet firmly on the ground.

The festival was only two days away and Tom was constantly monitoring for weather updates, desperate for nothing to dampen the big day. Luckily the forecast was dry and bright, but this didn't stop him from checking for any change. With the money they were going to make, he didn't want to leave anything to chance.

"Are you nervous?" asked Ricky.

"Honestly, no. Apprehensive yes," replied Tom. "I feel a responsibility for this to work, not just for the people who have bought tickets, but for you, Mum, Pope, and the people who've helped, like Carol and Mike. I need this, Ricky. Do you know what I mean? When I was in the city, working shitty jobs, I knew I could do something better, I knew I could do something important. This is my defining moment, and I need it to work, not just for the money, but for a bit of self-respect, something you and me can grow on."

"I am shitting myself!" replied Ricky. "Nice speech, by the way! Come on, let's go and get some lunch, and look at the dollar signs in Pope's eyes."

Fiona composed herself, and pushed her chair back in an attempt to distance herself. "Una does not want to see you. If you need to, I can make you an appointment."

"I do not want an appointment. I want to see Una now. Tell Una I am not going anywhere until I see her!"

Fiona knocked gently on her door trying to catch her attention. Una was on the phone, but became aware of Fiona slowly mouthing the words '*Clint... Lee,*' and pointing to the reception area. Una pulled a piece of notepaper while in mid-flow in conversation. She casually wrote on the paper, placed it neatly inside the envelope, and gestured for Fiona to take it. She turned her chair and returned her full attention to the phone call.

Fiona returned to the reception area, where she could smell Clint before she could see him. It wasn't a fresh alcohol smell, but rather a stale one, where days' worth of drinking seeps from every pore, clinging to the clothes. The stench of stale tobacco was overwhelming, and made Fiona gag, but Clint looked smart, and at first glance she couldn't believe this toxic aroma was emanating from the smartly dressed person sitting in front of her.

She assumed the envelope was a cheque, and passed it to Clint while desperately trying to maintain suitable distance. "Una is on the phone. She gave me this, for you." She had hoped he would take the envelope and leave, since she had clients due, and was desperate to open the windows and spray her perfume to mask the smell.

Clint looked puzzled, and opened the envelope, removing the note that had been carefully folded in four places. He smiled, and looked over toward Fiona before holding up the note.

In thick black pen, Una had neatly written: *FUCK YOU!!!*

Fiona tried to remain professional, but was unable to stifle a laugh, which was fortunately shared by Clint. He removed a flask from his inside pocket, and took a large mouthful.

"Please tell Una I'll wait."

"I assume he's still there?" Una shouted after several minutes. "I can smell him from here. Send him in, and call me

145

in three minutes to pretend I have another appointment." She said it loud enough for Clint to hear.

As Clint came in, she looked him up and down, and like Fiona, was surprised that he was smartly dressed. "Don't sit down, Clint. What do you want?"

Clint looked purposefully around the office at framed pictures of Una and her clients. "Your festival with The Overview looks like it's going quite well?"

Una knew exactly what Clint wanted, and didn't have time to play a game of verbal jousting. "Clint, save us both some time. You are getting *fuck-all* from this festival!"

"I have twenty K in that festival. Plus, I'm due thirty percent of what it makes!"

Una was no longer blunt or arrogant. She was angry with Clint. Angry at the time she had invested in him, and angry that he had destroyed a second chance, something most people do not get. "You sent some ageing gangster to see me! To get sixty thousand pounds that you owed him. Did you forget about that, you piece of shit?"

"I didn't mean to," mumbled Clint. "Besides, what I get from this I'll give to Larry."

"No you won't!" shouted Una. "You are getting nothing out of this. If you get any cash, you won't give it to Larry, you will either gamble it or piss it up against the wall. And when you do that, who do you think Larry will come and see, me or you? You have done nothing toward this. Christ, you were supposed to book the acts, and you couldn't even do *that* right. I am taking your twenty K, and giving it directly to Larry, and I will make up the shortfall. I will make it abundantly clear to him that I have nothing further to do with you, and if he is stupid enough to take any more bets off you, that is *his* problem."

Clint was taken aback. He had seen Una annoyed, but never like this. "Did Larry show you the little photographs I gave him? They were not the only copies!"

Una knew Clint was low, but she had not anticipated that he would stoop this low. The photographs were not pleasant, but they were not terminal. She had used them as leverage to get Paul to clean his act up, but other than some negative press, it wouldn't cause them any harm.

"I did," replied Una. "You know Paul Yorke better than me, and do you honestly think he will give a shit about this? He'll probably enjoy it."

Clint knew Una was right. Paul wouldn't care less if people saw a video of him naked with several women. The drugs were far from ideal, but it wouldn't be the end of his career. Clint was trying to play a game of verbal chess with the master, and knew he was destined to lose. He had lost everything, and this was one final desperate grasp at a payday.

Una would prefer that the photographs didn't get into the public domain, and knew that by throwing Clint a small lifeline, she may be able to achieve that. She knew that Larry would never do anything with the pictures, as long as she got his money, so the only potential leak would come from Clint.

"Clint, me and you are finished. That goes without saying. Other than a few people, no one really knows you've been drinking, and I can see to it that it stays out of the press. As I explained, I am keeping your money to clear your gambling debts. Call any excess my payment for keeping you out of the press. I had a call from Sol Brooks yesterday. He was asking about you for a role in his theatre. It isn't a massive role, but it is steady work, and if you clean yourself up, it could be a catalyst to other things."

Clint looked humbled. Getting back on the stage was all that he had wanted. He had assumed that his drinking would curtail any future work he could get. People knew his reputation, and he knew that if it got out in the press he was finished.

"Clint, I want you to get out of my office, and I don't want to see you again. You need to go home and have a shower, because you stink. I feel sick to my stomach at the moment. I will phone Sol Brooks and tell him that you'll be there tomorrow at ten a.m. You need to be sober and clean, and Clint, if you screw this up again, you are on your own. If I hear any whisper of these photographs being circulated, I will destroy you. Not only will I destroy your career, but I will pay your friend Larry another sixty K to make sure you don't walk straight."

Clint didn't say a word, but took an envelope containing the duplicate photographs, and placed it on her desk. "Thank you, Una."

Fiona was standing in the doorway of the office, as she'd heard the raised voices. She stepped aside as Clint left the office, deliberately holding her breath.

"Are you okay, Una?"

Una was shaken, but quickly composed herself. "I am now that idiot is out of my life. Phone Sol and tell him that Clint Lee is coming to see him tomorrow. Ask him to give him a role in his play, but something small. Mention that it's repayment for that thing I did for him last year. He'll know what you're talking about."

Una felt sorry for Clint, but she'd seen it all before. She had worked with a number of people who from the outside appeared to have it all. She could understand making a mistake once, but being given a second chance and throwing it away again was beyond stupid. She looked at the rise to fame that The Overview had experienced, and she often wondered whether this would lead to their ultimate downfall. It was for this reason that she would make acquaintances in this business and not friends, because regardless of their intentions, most of them would sooner or later let you down.

She smiled as she saw Fiona desperately spraying her perfume around the office to remove the acrid aroma that Clint had left behind. He was on his final chance, and for old times' sake, she hoped that he'd take it. She knew that if he didn't, there was only one outcome left for him, and she didn't want that.

She took the photographs from the envelope, and placed them over the shredder. She paused for a moment before slowly placing them back in the envelope. Opening her safe, she placed the envelope on top of a small pile of documents inside.

She smiled as she slammed the safe door shut.

Tom woke early, almost afraid to look at his watch, as sleep had become a rare commodity. He had been operating on adrenalin for weeks, but as the day arrived it was mixed with a range of emotions.

Carol was startled as he sat bolt upright before leaping out of bed. "You're like a child at Christmas," she joked. She knew there was little point in coercing him back into bed, because this was *his* day. He had been working toward it for weeks, and Carol was genuinely thrilled that she'd been part of the journey.

Tom had religiously checked the weather forecast, but was still relieved to step outside his log cabin to be met with a dry and bright morning. The tranquil surroundings had undergone a dramatic transformation, with security fencing forming a temporary blot on the landscape. It was difficult to comprehend that the serene backdrop before him would soon be invaded by over sixteen thousand people. A few short weeks ago, this outcome had been an aspiration, and a stern test of his wavering confidence.

Despite the early hour, a steady stream of technicians were making final adjustments to the stage, and security personnel had arrived at the start of what would be an exceptionally long day. Una had brought in a stage manager, and whilst Tom initially thought that this was an additional, unwarranted expense, the manager in question had been a revelation. Like Una, he was able to make quick decisions and resolve issues that Tom would have obsessed and worried over for hours. The entire experience had been a challenge for Tom, and he was starting to really understand the value of employing people who really knew their trade, people who had done this before and already learned from their mistakes.

Una had also been impressed. She was impressed with Tom, with his work ethic but more importantly his attitude. The event today was significant, but it wasn't just that which had occupied Tom's thoughts. It was the proposal that Una had given to him. Una was still relatively young, but she operated in a ruthless environment, one that rarely allowed for a long-term career. She had been looking for someone suitable, someone to compliment her business and also her personality. She viewed Tom as a rough diamond, one she could positively mould, as someone who had not already been poisoned by the business. He had been flattered when she'd asked him to join her. He was under no illusion that he would be the junior, but had the opportunity to be a partner in the business in a short space of time. He was concerned about Ricky and the campsite, but Una had given him assurances that he would have all the time that was required to grow the business. Una was keen to grow the music festival, and they'd already had detailed discussions about future events. Tom had ambition, he had the desire to grow it, but Una had the ability, and between them they could turn it into something special.

Tom enjoyed working with Ricky, but he was acutely aware that it wasn't difficult to manage the business on a day-to-day basis. Ricky was more than capable of doing it with a bit of assistance and oversight from him. The past few months working with his brother had been a major confidence boost for Tom, and confirmed his view that he was capable of doing something more with his life. He had harboured a concern that the campsite wouldn't offer a long-term challenge, and he knew that working with Una would provide that challenge he was looking for. He also knew that Carol for the most part enjoyed her career, and it was unlikely she'd be able to find any work in the country. Working with her would not only be a good career move, but it would also allow Tom to be with Carol full-time.

Una stepped into the luxurious black BMW, and sank into the deep leather passenger seat. It had been a difficult week for her, but she was relishing the trip to the countryside. Those that knew her would swear that Una was a city girl, but like most people, she had a deep affinity for the tranquillity of rural landscapes. She had no plans to stop working anytime soon, but when she did, moving to the countryside was a possibility.

The whole situation with Clint had been playing on her mind. She knew that she had been harsh on him in the past, but there was no denying that Clint was his own worst enemy. She smiled as The Overview played on the radio, and she discreetly sang along. The Overview and Clint were two extremes in terms of their career path, but they both shared the same destructive gene. It was something Una had seen numerous times, and it would never fail to frustrate her. However, she had long since given up trying to counsel people that were not willing to listen.

She thought about Tom, in particular his drive and magnetic enthusiasm, and hoped that he would take her up on her offer to come and work with her. She realised that she had a reputation that would make most people wary to work with her, but she knew she could collaborate well with Tom, and got the impression that he was willing to work hard.

The journey to the country was a long one, and Una was not one to relax, but the lack of a phone signal, and miles of road before her, meant a rare opportunity to switch off. She looked at her handsome companion and smiled, placing her hand gently on his.

She had experienced people in place to ensure today ran without issue, but she still felt an element of apprehension. It was not just an important day for her biggest client, but the event was a commercial success, so it was vital that it ran without any issues. She had been sceptical that the event would work, as there was a lot of competition in that space. It was an area she had not been involved in before, but the success of this one meant that she was very keen to develop the event, and turn it into an annual one, which she would hopefully work on with Tom.

As they drove through Tinsbury, Una, like most, was captivated by its beauty. The usually sedate village was now teeming with people generating a party atmosphere. It was slow progress working through the narrow roads to the rapidly filling car parks. It was not often that Una was overwhelmed, but the sheer flow of people brought a smile to her face. They parked the car, and her door opened. The driver extended a gracious arm, which Una gratefully accepted. She stepped out of the car and placed a gentle kiss on his cheek. "Thank you, Larry."

Pope had been up since first light, and like Tom, hadn't slept for days. He had to pinch himself that he was involved, and it had been an experience he would never forget. When Tom asked him to put money into the idea, he was sceptical, and was buying into Tom rather than the event. He had known Tom for years, but had only really got to truly know him since he'd returned to the village. Pope would have been happy to just get his money back, but with the amount of tickets they had sold he was in line for a big payday. He wasn't motivated by money, but the truth was that this event would help him and his business. The pub trade had been suffering for years, and in a small village he was not immune. There were a finite number of customers, and he had previously broached the unthinkable thought that he would need to leave the village if things didn't pick up. Tom returning to the village had brought a real change in fortune for the pub, and with the money from the festival it looked like it would secure its long-term future. It wasn't just Pope; the whole village had an eager buzz about it. People that he thought would be vehemently opposed to the event had long since come around, as it placed the village on the map, and would bring much-needed income. Tom had already told Pope that he was thinking about repeating the event next year. Pope had contributed little other than money and enthusiasm, and whilst he relished being involved, he assumed that his involvement would only be for this year. Tom slapped Pope down when he heard this, because he had no intention of cutting him out if they chose to run the event again. Tom had been an unknown entity, and the festival could have failed miserably, but regardless of this, Pope had shown real faith in Tom, and it was a faith that he was eager to repay. Una was a little reluctant when Tom had mentioned this, but soon understood and respected the loyalty that he was showing.

Pope had opened the doors to the pub at 8 a.m. and it had been full all morning. He was determined to enjoy the day, so had employed extra staff to allow him to fully immerse himself in the proceedings. It was a beautifully warm day, the beer garden was full to bursting, and he had reluctantly placed the 'doors full' sign up not long after opening. It was strictly one-in-one-out, but Pope was satisfying demand with a temporary beer kiosk. He had been in the pub game for years, but this was crazy, and he was determined to enjoy every minute of it.

Ricky stood with the security staff, watching as an endless stream of people handed over their tickets. As he looked at the queue, he had a feeling of immense pride knowing that this was something he was involved with, something he had made happen. He'd been hesitant when Tom first announced that he was coming home, and knew the campsite was barely surviving, which had been a real blow to his sense of pride. He was concerned that Tom would place the blame on him, and make him feel like a failure, but his concerns had been misplaced. He had learned a lot from his brother, and since he came back, he had his own home, and for once he had no concerns about money.

He enjoyed working with Tom, but he doubted whether his brother would stay in the countryside forever. He had made the break once, and he felt that once the novelty had worn off, Tom would return to the City. Carol and Tom were getting closer, and he doubted whether Carol would move to the city, but he figured that they would make good rental money from the cabin if they did leave.

All of the acts had arrived, and were now safely backstage, which meant that Ricky could relax. His main concern was that The Overview might let them down at the last minute. It wouldn't have been a disaster if one of the other bands didn't arrive, but if The Overview didn't show up it would have been terminal. He had little doubt the other bands wouldn't show up, as the event was bigger than they were used to, and would likely serve as a catalyst to rejuvenate their careers.

Tom, Mike and Carol stood on the porch of the cabin, watching the orderly chaos unfold in front of them. Like Ricky, Tom felt that he could relax for the first time. Carol looked at Tom and could see the glimmer in his eyes, and she shared his immense pride.

"Come on!" said Tom. "Let's go and enjoy this!"

The first act burst into life bang on schedule, and the noise was deafening. Tom had heard a brief soundcheck, but this was on a different level. Instantly the crowd turned to the stage, and were swept up in the atmosphere.

Tom pretended to put his fingers in his ears, and gestured that they go for a pint, which was met with warm approval. The queue in the beer tent had disappeared once the first act started, and Tom eagerly ordered a round of drinks. He raised his plastic glass and smiled at Carol and Mike. "If you really want it, you will find a way. If you don't, you will find an excuse."

"Very deep!" said Carol, raising her glass.

"No, I just decided I was going to stop finding an excuse and do something. And guys, thank you. Thank you for being a part it."

Carol and Mike leaned forward and shared a hug with him. It was a special moment for Tom, who had thought about this day for weeks, and now it was here he felt fantastic. It was like everything he had hoped for.

Ricky walked in proudly. "Here he is!" shouted Mike.

"That band is a bit shit, but they seem to love it. Cheers!" said Ricky, as he took Tom's pint out of his hand.

Tom ordered himself another drink, and took a deep breath. "Mike, Ricky, I need to tell you something."

"You're gay?" suggested Ricky.

"He better not be!" said Carol.

"How old are you?" said Tom with a grin. "The thing is, Una has offered me a job. Well, more of a junior partnership, and, well, it means that I will need to move back to the city."

"Good, I can get a hundred quid a night for that cabin," replied Ricky. "Plus, you were a shit neighbour!"

"So you don't mind?" asked Tom.

"No, not at all, I was half expecting it, to be honest."

"Good, just don't cock things up, though, because me and Carol need somewhere to spend our weekends!" Tom turned to Mike. "Mike, I spoke with Una," he said. "And if you're up for it, there's plenty of work? She's a bit of a ball-breaker, but fine once you get to know her."

Mike smiled and nodded. "Mate, that would be great, thank you!"

Tom looked toward the entrance of the beer tent. "Speaking of Una, there she is now."

"I didn't know she was married?" asked Carol.

Tom could see that she was walking through the crowd, holding hands with someone. "She isn't. Well, I don't think she is. To be honest, I thought she was, well, you know, more Martha than Arthur."

Tom looked shocked. "Holy shit, that's Larry she's with!"

"Larry, as in *Larry*?" asked Mike.

Tom nodded. "Yeah, that's Larry alright. I'm looking forward to finding out how that one came about!"

"Maybe getting a bit will chill her out?" said Carol.

Tom laughed. "Maybe! Larry is braver than I thought!"

The afternoon disappeared in a blur, as a steady stream of local and established bands took to the stage. Some of the acts were not as refined as others, but a mix of alcohol and a beautiful summer's day meant that the crowd were somewhat forgiving.

As the evening approached, the sense of anticipation grew, as it meant that The Overview would soon be onstage. Tom had enjoyed a couple of pints, but had deliberately remained sober, as he wanted to enjoy the day. Tom and the others moved toward the VIP area to the front of the stage, where they saw Pope, who had evidently been enjoying the beer tent longer than they had.

Carol laughed, and waved to Pope, who'd started to remove his shirt. The security staff quickly intercepted, and politely requested that he remain fully clothed.

Tom looked back toward the crowd, and could see an ocean of smiling heads looking up toward the stage. He took his phone out and took a picture, so he could look back on the scale of the event. The crowd surged forward, and he momentarily panicked as The Overview took to the stage. It was as if everyone in the crowd had pulled out their phones and cameras in unison, and he was almost blinded by the constant flashes. People had enjoyed the day so far, but it was a prelude to this, and the noise was incredible.

The Overview were seasoned professionals, and they knew how to work the crowd, who loved it. Tom took a bottle of champagne and handed out the glasses. At that moment, Una walked toward him and reached for a glass. It was loud, so she didn't try to speak. She stared intently at Tom. Her usual stern expression gave way to a warm smile, and she nodded in admiration. She took a slow look around at the stage, the band and the crowd, before looking back at Tom, and pointing to him. He was responsible for all of this.

The champagne flowed as Tom and Carol danced away the evening in the VIP section. The Overview were world-class, and Tom knew this was a special night. As the band reached the end of their set, Una walked toward him and took him by the hand, out toward the rear of the stage. She flashed her security pass, and was escorted up to the side of the stage. The view from here was even more spectacular, and you could really get a sense of the scale of the festival.

The band sang their final song, and the crowd erupted as they walked from the stage to where Tom and Una were standing. It was impossible to hear anything over the crowd, and after a couple of minutes the band returned to the stage to acknowledge their fans. As they walked into the bright lights, Una walked behind them and grabbed Tom by the hand. Tom froze to the spot and pulled back, terrified by the prospect of walking out in front of all of those people. Una looked at him reassuringly and gently pulled her toward him.

"This is for you!" she shouted.

He reluctantly walked out onto the stage, and was instantly overwhelmed. The Overview graciously accepted the adoration of the crowd.

Paul Yorke was handed a microphone. "Thank you. Thank you all for making this an amazing night." The crowd erupted again, and the camera flashes started all over again. "You are what make us. Without you we are nothing."

Tom's legs had turned to jelly, and he could just make out Carol standing at the foot of the stage.

"We hope you enjoyed today. We want to thank our manager, Una, who's helped us through some difficult times. We also want to introduce you to our special friend, Tom, because without him today wouldn't have happened."

Paul pointed toward Tom, who genuinely thought his legs were going to buckle. He managed a wave toward the crowd, and was totally overwhelmed by the moment. He looked in horror as Paul handed him the microphone, which he clutched with terror. It seemed like hours passed as he stared blankly at the crowd before him.

He took a deep breath. "I just want to thank you all for making my dream become a reality." His voice was now audibly shaking. "Should we do another one next year?" he shouted.

It was evident from the noise that today had been a real success, as Una gave him a gentle pat on the back. He looked down, and could see Carol jumping and waving with a huge smile on her face. He walked forward a little and pointed toward Carol. "I just wanted to thank my beautiful girlfriend for everything. She's my life!"

He paused for a moment and looked stunned as he quickly dropped on one knee. "Carol, will you marry me?"

The crowd went ballistic as Carol blew a kiss and frantically nodded her head.

Paul moved toward Tom, clapping his hands as he took the microphone back. "She said yes!" He waved at the crowd. "We will see you all next year!"

Tom ran from the stage toward Carol, who was waiting for him at the bottom of the stairs. He paused for a moment to gauge her reaction, but it was quickly evident that she was delighted. He moved toward her as she desperately tried to wipe away tears from her eyes. Mike and Ricky ran over and jumped on Tom, nearly dropping him to the floor.

"I love you, Carol."

As soon as the band finished, the crowd started to disappear back toward the car parks. It was surreal to now look around and see a virtually empty field that had been bustling shortly before. Tom didn't want to see the crew dismantling the stage, as he didn't want anything to dampen his enjoyment of the day. Seeing everything being removed would feel like how a child feels when the Christmas decorations are taken down in January.

He required little coercion to continue the party back at his cabin, despite wanting to spend some time alone with Carol. The day had been a huge success, and there was an overwhelming sense of achievement, and people naturally wanted to congratulate Tom, both for his engagement and also the success of the day.

He was pleased that Una had agreed to join them, as he'd started to see a side to her beyond the ice maiden persona. He was desperate to know how she and Larry had become so friendly, but he thought that conversation best suited to a sober occasion. He did take the opportunity to ask Larry what had happened to the bloke that ran Mike over.

Larry put his arm around Tom. "Don't you worry about him, son, he won't bother you or your friend anymore!"

Tom looked relieved although the outcome was never in doubt. "Did you, well, you know…?"

"No, son, no need. He was psychotic, and I had to admire that in him. I gave him a job."

Pope had been smiling since Tom had seen him at first light, and despite succumbing to the alcohol and the late hour, he was still enjoying every minute of the day.

It was a time to relax for Tom, as he'd been carrying a weight of burden for as long as he could remember. The day had gone without incident, other than people being ejected for drinking too much, or smoking something they shouldn't have. He smiled as he saw Ricky dancing with Carol, and Mike dancing with his mum. This is what Tom wanted; he wanted everything to work out and for people to have smiles on their faces. He was pleased that Lou had accepted his invite and even more so as she had come alone. He didn't harbour any animosity and if anything, he wanted to show her what he had achieved.

Those looking at Tom may have mistaken his demeanour as nonchalance, but he was simply absorbing the moment, watching and enjoying those closest to him.

It was a special moment for him and one that he would never forget. He felt proud of himself and it felt fantastic.

Tom and Carol were awake early, keen to get the car packed up and make the long journey back to the city. Una had suggested that he take a few days before starting his new job, but Tom was eager to jump into his new role. The new opportunity in the city was slightly tinged in sadness, as it meant him leaving the village again, but he had committed to returning on a more frequent basis. He sat in the car and cringed at the aftermath of the night before, as the campsite looked like it had been hit by a tornado. He knew that the business was in capable hands, and Ricky had agreed to share the burden and reach out if he needed any assistance.

Carol fastened her seatbelt and looked over to Tom. "You're quiet this morning. Is everything alright? No second thoughts, I hope?"

Tom smiled. It was the opposite, and as he looked at Carol he knew that there was no place on earth he would rather be.

"I'm fine, honest, in fact better than fine, better than I have been for a long time! Come on, let's get this show on the road!"

As they drove out of the village, he thought about the last time he'd decided to leave, and reflected on the difference in emotions. He was starting a new chapter in his life, one filled with opportunity and with someone to share the journey with, someone he wanted to wake up next to every day.

He thought back to the day when he'd finally decided to do something, and how that one decision had made such an impact on his life. There had been risks, albeit calculated risks, but without them, his life would not have changed, and he would have continued on a downward spiral.

This time Tom was leaving as a success, a pillar of the community, who had made a real difference to people's lives.

This time Tom was leaving with something that money could not buy. He was leaving with pride and hope.

The End

Other Books by JC Williams

If you've enjoyed this book, the author would be very grateful if you would be so kind as to leave feedback on Amazon. You can subscribe for author updates and news on new releases at:

www.authorjcwilliams.com

J C Williams
Author

authorjcwilliams@gmail.com
🐦 @jcwilliamsbooks
📘 @jcwilliamsauthor

And if you've enjoyed this book, make sure to check out my other books as well!

The *Frank 'n' Stan's Bucket List* series:

The Lonely Heart Attack Club series, with the third instalment, *The Lonely Heart Attack Club: Project VIP*, coming soon!

The Seaside Detective Agency

And you may also wish to check out my other books aimed at a younger audience...

Cabbage von Dagel *Hamish McScabbard*

Luke 'n' Conor's Hundred-to-One Club
and
Deputy Gabe Rashford: Showdown at Buzzards Creek

All jolly good fun! And also…

For the *very* adventurous among you, you may wish to give my hardworking editor's most peculiar book a butcher's. Lavishly illustrated by award-winning artist Tony Millionaire of *Maakies* and *Sock Monkey* fame.

Recommended for readers age 14 and up.

Printed in Great Britain
by Amazon